LIVING TRANSLATION

Peace Children – The Sawi Story

Bruce A. Smith

XULON PRESS

Xulon Press
2301 Lucien Way #415
Maitland, FL 32751
407.339.4217
www.xulonpress.com

Unless otherwise indicated, Scripture quotations taken from the Holy Bible, New International Version (NIV). Copyright © 1973, 1978, 1984, 2011 by Biblica, Inc.™. Used by permission. All rights reserved.

Printed in the United States of America.

ISBN-13: 978-1-6305-0196-9

TABLE OF CONTENTS

PREFACE

I n February 2000, the Wycliffe Associates Board invited me to become President of our ministry advancing Bible translation. After three years working with our team in Southern California, it was clear that God was moving the ministry in a new direction both physically and strategically. So, Jan and I moved from California to Florida. As a result of this move, a couple years later my life changed in a very unexpected way.

One evening I walked out my front door to go for a run. Before I had a chance to get moving, another runner came toward me. He paused at the end of my driveway to introduce himself, "Hi. I'm Don Richardson." My heart rate accelerated—even though I was standing still! I couldn't believe it. I had just met Don Richardson. He was my neighbor!

I first heard the name Don Richardson when I was in the Missions degree program at LeTourneau College back in 1975. Don's first book, *Peace Child*, had just been published and was required reading for my missions anthropology class. Everything about this unique missionary memoir fascinated me. I was impressed by the Sawi people and by the Richardson family, who moved to Indonesia to learn the Sawi language and culture so they could translate the New Testament into their heart language. It was one of the many times in my life that I wished I had been born a generation earlier. Don had done what I dreamed of doing.

It has now been 14 years since I met Don. During those years we became good friends. He became a Barnabas to me. He wrote an endorsement for my first book. He traveled thousands of miles and spoke dozens of times at Wycliffe Associates events across the United States. He lent his reputation and experience to encourage others to support Bible translation in partnership with us. We spent many hours together in conversation, reflection, and prayer. Every moment was a priceless treasure for me.

In March 2018 Jan and I were at Mayo Clinic caring for our daughter, Lindsey, following surgery. I received an email telling me that Don had surgery in Orlando to remove a brain tumor. My already weary heart skipped a few beats. I was in shock. When Jan and I returned to Orlando a few weeks later, we stopped by to visit Don and Carol. By then the diagnosis was confirmed. Don had a glioblastoma. They were weighing the pros and cons of various treatment options. The pros were few, and the cons were many. Either way, Don knew his days were numbered by God.

Three months later I was sitting in the audience, watching an award ceremony unfold. Don was being honored with a Lifetime of Service Award. The presenter described Don's impact on Christian missions at length in appropriate superlatives. How do you honor and recognize a lifetime of influence on thousands of missionaries impacting hundreds of millions of people worldwide? The presenter handed Don a plaque, and my heart sank.

As Don took the podium and reflected on his lifetime in missions, I soaked in every word. I knew I was listening to a missionary statesman. During Don's address, I leaned over to whisper to my friend and colleague Brent Ropp, "There must be a better way to honor Don's lifetime of work." That got Brent thinking.

When the ceremony ended a few minutes later, Don was immediately surrounded by a crowd. As Brent and I drifted toward the hallway, he said, "What if we help the Sawi finish the translation of their Bible? That would be more meaningful than giving Don a plaque."

As soon as I heard Brent's question, several thoughts converged in my brain. First, over the 33 years Brent and I had worked together in ministry, this kind of interaction has happened hundreds of times—often leading to unprecedented and unimagined breakthroughs in ministry. I knew from experience that God was speaking through Brent. Second, because Don had spent his lifetime working to advance the gospel and Bible translation in every language, I knew this would be a fitting tribute and encouragement to him. Third, without knowing how much time Don would have on earth, the only way this could happen would be for the Sawi to mobilize a large number of bilingual translators within a short period of time. Fourth, I knew that only God could make it happen.

God did make it happen. That is the rest of the story.

DEDICATION

This book is dedicated to the growing body of Christians worldwide who are working daily to assure that no one is beyond the reach of God's Word in their heart language.

This story is a testimony to the power of the seed of God's Word, the fruitfulness of the Sawi soil, and the faithfulness of Don Richardson as the pioneer sower in this field.

ACKNOWLEDGMENTS

This story would be unknown except for the extraordinary grace of the Sawi people. It was first written in their lives. They invited and welcomed foreigners into their community and into their story. Their grace overflows from the grace they receive from God's hand. Their Christian testimony is salt and light in Papua, across Indonesia, and around the world.

Don Richardson similarly invited me into his story. His experience and ideas shaped my ministry perspectives. He introduced me to his family and friends. He encouraged me to connect with the Sawi, walk where he walked, and give my voice to tell their story. He shared his time with me even as it was becoming more precious and tenuous.

Don's wife, Carol Joyce, was closely involved from the inception of this book until its completion. She provided expert editorial feedback, careful corrections to my factual misunderstandings, and thoughtful counsel at key decision points along the way.

Don's son, Steve, encouraged me throughout this effort and reviewed the manuscript despite overflowing demands on his time.

The extended Wycliffe Associates family was also indispensable to writing this book. Our convergence with the Sawi was written in their hearts and lives. They responded graciously to my endless questions and provided invaluable corrections and details to get the story right. I want to especially recognize Christov, Yanti, Sierra, and Wesly for their work in Papua and throughout Indonesia. Dan Kramer, the creator of MAST, built the foundation of this movement and continues to manage ongoing MAST training and innovation worldwide. Brent Ropp, my partner in ministry across four decades, leads our global Operations team as we serve the church. Tabitha Price lent her experienced editorial voice to improve my storytelling and eliminate distractions. Cindy Gray created the cover design from an original painting by Don Richardson titled *A Man of Peace Pleads* (used with permission: https://www.peacechildlegacy.com/).

Living and writing this story would be impossible for me without the support and encouragement of my wife, Jan, and daughters, Abby and Lindsey. Jan journeyed with me to the Sawi swamp and inspires me to continue serving. Abby and Lindsey would have loved to travel to meet the Sawi but instead cheered us on from their homes with their loving families. Abby provided insightful editorial feedback as only a daughter can do.

Despite the best efforts of all these people, errors may have inadvertently persisted in my writing. For that, I accept sole responsibility and apologize in advance.

Endorsements

" I have a deep and abiding love for 'my people'—the Sawi tribe. Having been raised among them, our stories will forever be interwoven. Their embrace of the gospel has inspired the global church. The faith of Sawi believers has endured, and their language and culture preserved, in large measure I believe because they received the New Testament in their own language as an early priority. Now to see them pursue the Old Testament as well, and to embrace their part in the Great Commission, brings overflowing joy!"

Steve Richardson
President, Pioneers-USA

"For over six decades the late Don Richardson worked to further the Gospel globally. The joy he experienced in translating scripture into the Sawi language and seeing its indispensable role in planting churches among tribal peoples became a lifelong impetus for promoting Bible translation. His book *Peace Child* told the 'original story' of God's amazing work among the Sawi tribe. *Living Translation: Peace Children— The Sawi Story* narrates a gripping, eternity-impacting continuation of that story. I commend this detailed case history as one that not only opens readers' understanding of the work of one Bible translation agency but also reinforces the main reason such work is so important: access to God's Word in one's 'heart language' is indisputably the greatest asset and treasure for growth in personal discipleship and corporate mission among God's people. Bravo, Bruce! Thank You, Lord!"

Carol Richardson, servant of Jesus Christ,
and Don Richardson's widow

"History is His-story, The Great Commission will be done no matter whether we decide to obey or not. This book will show you that when you obey, God will lead you along the way. To God be the Glory!"

Christov Manuhutu
Managing Director, Bahasa Technology
Solutions—Indonesia

"This book is a great reference for the mission world in this modern era to see the journey of a tribe from a world of tribal war and cannibalism, to becoming Christians, then finally becoming pioneers of Bible translation in the South of Papua. As a witness to some of the events in this book, I directly saw how Bruce documented well the testimony of key actors of the story, eating and laughing with them, and closely touching them—which makes this book feel alive! This book is one of the best gifts of the mission world for Papua."

Jhon Wesly Marthinus Raunsay
Papua MAST Coordinator, Bahasa Technology
Solutions—Indonesia

Introduction

I trained in college as a pilot and aircraft mechanic. In 1978 I married my high school sweetheart. After college graduation, Jan and I volunteered for a summer with Mission Aviation Fellowship in Suriname, South America. It was Jan's first time outside the U.S. It was my second overseas experience, having spent one summer with Teen Missions International building a church in rural northwestern Guatemala after high school. These were deeply formative experiences for us.

We worked among people who lived very simply. They had very limited access to education, medicine, or modern conveniences—not by choice but because of location and circumstance. During our summer in Suriname we visited the Wayana tribe in the northern Amazon jungle. One experience during that visit is indelibly etched in my mind.

The tribe lived on the shore of a rushing river. There were stretches where the placid water swelled and pooled, but there were also stretches of boiling rapids as the water crashed against rocks that were mostly concealed beneath the cola-colored water and foam. In the heat of the day, the children played in the water. One after another, we saw them leap into the pool, submerge under the surface, then careen down the rapids! As they tumbled through the turmoil, occasionally an arm or leg would be briefly visible. Just when I thought they would run out of breath, they would surface below the rapids smiling and laughing raucously. Jan must have seen the foolishness in my eyes. "Don't you dare!" she ordered. I wanted to jump in the river and have the ride of my life but she, rightly, judged that it could be the last ride of my life!

How could it be safe for those kids to dive into the river but not for me? I was bigger, stronger, and smarter—I thought. But therein lay the secret. I was not smarter. I had a college degree, but they were born on the river. They had consciously and unconsciously studied it every day of their lives. They had walked on those boulders during the dry season when only a small trickle of water moistened the sand between them. They watched the torrent build when the rains began upstream. They saw boulders broken and moved by the relentless flood. They started swimming in the river as soon as they could walk, when they were small and buoyant. As they grew older, they bruised their shins, hips, and heads enough to learn the best routes for navigation—and survival.

They knew secrets about their river that no outsider would ever learn.

Six years—and two daughters—later we joined Mission Aviation Fellowship (MAF) full-time. I was anxious to use my aviation training and experience to help reach the least-reached people of the world with the good news of the gospel. We arrived at MAF the same month that their long-time CEO, Chuck Bennett, handed over the reins of leadership to a new man. It is quite possible that I heard Chuck speak publicly only one time, but I remember exactly what he said. "There is a day coming when the local Christians will be ready, willing, and able to take full responsibility and lead every aspect of Christian ministry in their nations." With my nearly complete lack of experience, I had no way to understand his statement. I didn't know who, what, when, where, why, or how this could happen. We were heading out into the great unknown—at least it was unknown to us. I should have remembered the lesson from the children in Suriname, but I didn't.

In God's providence, our first assignment with MAF was back to Suriname. Wholly unrelated to our arrival, a civil war promptly began there. The first thing the government did was ground MAF. The government was centered in the capital city of Paramaribo. The rebels were dispersed throughout the interior jungle. The government wanted to make absolutely sure MAF was not aiding the rebellion. After a few months fixing and polishing our small fleet, I asked for something else to do while we were grounded. MAF reassigned us to Haiti.

It was January 1987. Baby Doc Duvalier, Haiti's dictator, had been ousted eleven months previously. MAF, and our family, stepped into the anarchy to provide air transpor‑ tation for missionaries, local pastors, and humanitarian workers. Again, unrelated to our arrival (I like to think), the MAF family that preceded us in Haiti departed—and never returned! I joined Haitian colleagues who spoke no English, and I spoke no Creole. I also knew absolutely nothing about Haiti, neither its recent history nor its distant past. I knew nothing about the missionaries, nothing about the churches, nothing about the people, and nothing about how to live and work in Haiti. But Willy did.

Willy was born in Port au Prince the same year I was born in Hammond, Indiana. He had lived his entire life in Haiti. In fact, he had never been outside Haiti's borders. He was a brother in Christ, and he taught me most of what I learned during our four years there. He taught me to speak, and to think, in Creole. Soon I became fluent enough to get myself in and out of trouble predictably. But at no time did I ever entertain the delusion that I knew Creole, or Haiti, better than Willy did. He was always the expert. I was always the student.

More than two decades later, about twelve years into my full-time focus on advancing Bible translation with Wycliffe Associates (WA), one of our international partners stopped by my Orlando office for a conversation. When he asked if he could close the door, I knew he was serious. He said, "I want to tell you about a conversation we're having among several international leaders in Bible translation." I was all ears. We had been partnering closely with these leaders and organizations since before my arrival at WA, and my respect for them was high.

"We've decided it's time for us to have a gathering of international Bible translation leaders... without any Americans or Europeans present."

These men and women had spent their entire careers under the overpowering influence of Americans and Europeans, and they felt it was time for global South leaders to sharpen one another without wondering about what Big Brother was thinking.

"I think it's a GREAT idea!" I responded.

"Good, because we'd like you to join us."

"No. I'm part of the problem. You need to meet without worrying about what I'm hearing or thinking."

"We've already decided. You need to come."

I was in a cross-cultural corner. Out of respect for these leaders, I had to accept their invitation. But I still had an opportunity to negotiate the terms.

"If I come, I will not be part of the planning. I will not make any presentations from the podium. I will sit in the back row, listening and praying."

"That's why we want you to come."

So, I went. I saw the agenda priorities they chose. I heard their unguarded conversations about the challenges and opportunities they faced in Bible translation. I heard them counsel and pray with each other. And, in the back row, I remembered what Chuck Bennett had said almost thirty years before. Suddenly I realized that the future day Chuck had described was already past. These men and women were expertly leading Bible translation in their nations. I was welcome, even invited, but I was not the expert. They were, and are, the experts. We foreigners are the students.

For most of the past century, Bible translation has been controlled by foreigners. Western missionaries moved into remote villages with foreign resources and a plan. The missionaries became students of the language and culture, then translated Scripture through their foreign understanding of the local language. The local language experts—those who spoke it as their mother tongue—were grateful to have Scripture for the first time. But too often, after using the Scripture, they realized the shortcomings of the foreigner's translation. They were willing to correct the translation problems, but many times learned that they needed someone's permission to revise their copyrighted Bible. When permission to revise wasn't forthcoming, some churches even developed customized local seminary training to teach pastors how to preach around the known translation weaknesses in their Bible. They felt trapped.

Then something changed. The language experts, the local Christians, decided they were going to do Bible translation themselves. Wycliffe Associates developed Mobilized Assistance Supporting Translation (MAST) to support them in this work. At first it was just a few languages scattered among the hinterlands of the world. Then the word spread. Nearby languages heard that their neighbors had translated Scripture themselves, and they learned how to do Bible translation from the other's experience. A few became a few dozen, then a few hundred. I told some of the earliest stories of MAST in my previous book *Living Translation: Their Stories*. During the last five years churches in more than 1,500 languages have launched Bible translations using MAST. Every indication is that this trend will continue until every language in the world has God's Word.

I know many people who have prayed, worked, and given for this to happen throughout their entire lives. This movement is a tremendous answer to prayer—but it may not be exactly the answer we expected. We may not have realized that God

1

A DIFFERENT WORLD

The world was a very different place in 1962.

The space race and the cold war were escalating. The USA was beginning to close the gap on the USSR's lead in space as John Glenn orbited the earth. President John F. Kennedy imposed a trade embargo on Cuba to put pressure on the Communist regime, and the USSR responded by building nine ballistic missile bases in Cuba capable of reaching almost any location in the USA. After narrowly avoiding war, a telephone hotline was established between Washington and Moscow to improve communications.

The war in Vietnam was in its seventh year, growing more complicated and more costly by the day. With an escort of US Marshals, James Meredith became the first black student to attend the University of Mississippi. The Space Needle observation tower became the symbolic landmark of the World's Fair held in Seattle.

Sam Walton opened the first Walmart. The Beatles released their first song. Spiderman made his first appearance in Marvel Comics. Marilyn Monroe was found dead from a drug overdose. Johnny Carson began hosting The Tonight Show, and Walter Cronkite started delivering the CBS Evening News.

Global population was just a little more than half of today's population. European colonial powers finally recognized the national independence of Algeria, Burundi, Jamaica, Trinidad and Tobago, Uganda, and Western Samoa. Nelson Mandela was arrested and jailed for inciting rebellion in South Africa. Pope John XXIII convened Vatican II. Scientists James D. Watson and Francis H. C. Crick won the Nobel Prize in medicine for determining the chemical structure of DNA. Britain and France agreed to develop the Concorde supersonic transport airplane.

According to the *World Christian Database*, in 1900 there were fewer than 94 million Christians globally outside of Europe and North America. Because of Christian missionaries, by 1962 that population had grown to approximately 450 million.

Meanwhile, on the remote southern coast of then Netherlands New Guinea, ruthless men and women were killing, dismembering, and eating their enemies.

The Sawi were cannibals in 1962.

LIVING IN FEAR

Pervasive Fear

For untold generations the Sawi world was filled with fear.

From childhood, men were taught to be wary of everything and everyone. The water and the forest were filled with natural and supernatural threats. Wild animals, swirling river currents, and poisonous plants guarded the forest's wealth. Words could not be trusted. Friends and even relatives were always suspect, their allegiance potentially evaporating in a cloud of treachery. Strangers, neighboring villagers, or distant enemies could appear unexpectedly, turning a daydream into a nightmare. Constant vigilance was required to survive.

Women feared all these same things, but in addition lived in fear of their husbands and their other wives. Tempers flared unpredictably, scorching anyone within reach. Favoritism and neglect varied capriciously, along with physical and sexual abuse.

Pervasive fear required every Sawi to sharpen his offense and defense. Suspicion and deception rose to the level of high art. Young boys were schooled in the lethal art of killing. Young girls were prohibited from having weapons of war but learned how to improvise their own defense with farming tools or whatever sticks and rocks were within reach.

Hearts of both men and women were battle-hardened by chronic loss and betrayal.

A Sawi elder described it to me recently. "I remember being surrounded by fear. I was afraid of my father. I was afraid of my grandfather and my uncles. When they were angry, I fled from them. When they were not angry, I held my breath in anticipation of what might trigger the next violent outburst."

Demonic Power

Cannibalism was their darkest sin. The Sawi knew the reputation and conquests of each of their warriors. Bare skulls hung from rafters, stood on spearheads, and pillowed warriors' heads as grim reminders of the threat to every living person. This could be you. It was no idle threat. Every skull had a name.

Cannibalism was also a human response to demonic influence. It was the ultimate appeasement for demons bent on the destruction of humanity. When amulets and fetishes failed to constrain demonic action, cannibalism would satisfy their evil appetite—until it would not, and they demanded more.

Feast and Flood

For generations the forest provided for the Sawi. Tropical rain and sunshine meant that every living thing would grow. Wild animals provided protein, fruits yielded vitamins, and vegetables offered minerals and starch. The forest's abundant resources supported the Sawi hunters and gatherers.

But, unpredictably, too much sun or rain would flood their world. Too much sun would scorch and wither the fruits of the jungle. Too much rain would drive the animals further into the bush and wash the fruits downstream in a torrent.

An Outsider Arrives

Into this world, Don and Carol Richardson, Christian missionaries with Regions Beyond Missionary Union, arrived with their infant son, Stephen, in July 1962.

Their arrival was like a magnet for the Sawi. Families from distant Sawi villages resettled near Kamur village in order to be near *Tuan* (Sir) Don. He was an outsider with unknown powers and resources that beckoned to be explored and exploited. The Sawi knew nothing of Don's motives for coming but had plenty of their own selfish reasons for inviting and welcoming the Richardsons to Kamur.

The patriarch of the Tumdu River, Hato, was the Richardsons' neighbor. Hato had lost one eye to an arrow years before, but his remaining eye missed nothing. Kigo, one of the head men of Kamur, used his position and influence to stay close by. Young couples like Kaiyo and Wumi wondered how their families might benefit from close proximity to *Tuan* Don.

The master of treachery from Haenam village, Kani, moved closer to protect his interests. Kani's close allies from

Haenam—Mahaen and Toh—gradually insinuated their way into *Tuan* Don's circle.

As soon as Don arrived, he focused on two priorities: building a house and learning the Sawi language. It took a while for the Sawi to understand Don's gestures and expressions, but before long they grasped his goals and rallied alongside him to help him achieve them.

It would not take Don long to learn more about the Sawi world than he ever imagined.

3

WHAT HAPPENED?

Hollow Victory

The Sawi were well known among neighboring tribes as ruthless killers. Competition for scarce natural resources was a life-or-death battle and the Sawi were experts at eliminating rivals. Few outside the Sawi knew that among themselves, within their extended and overlapping families, their violence was equally fierce. Insults, thievery, lies, and infidelity kept the Sawi at each others' throats.

As payback for his brother's murder, Kani engineered a diabolical scheme to take the lives of the men responsible. His genius was in blackmailing Mahaen to deceive the killers—Mahaen's own cousins. But despite the public adulation he received for his crucial role in Kani's revenge, privately Mahaen felt crushing darkness in his soul. He had done what was required. But secretly he felt trapped and betrayed by Kani. He had dutifully played his part in the conspiracy, betraying his own cousins to a horrible death.

The mangled and decapitated bodies of his four cousins lay decomposing on the ground, the main course in the cannibal feast of celebration. Their blood mixed in puddles at the feet of the dancers. But amid the community celebration of this new pinnacle of treachery, Mahaen had no appetite. Having done everything prescribed and expected, he knew it was all for naught. Kani's revenge vented his boiling anger, but it didn't reduce his grief for his brother. The men and women of Haenam celebrated Mahaen, but he knew the men of Wasohwi would respond by escalating the violence. Victory was always hollow and fleeting.

While others danced in wild revelry, Mahaen broke away from the crowd and walked back to the men's house alone. It was empty, and so was he. In the weeks and months to come, the routines of life brought some measure of peace to his aching soul. A year later his wife gave birth to another son, Mani. He brought new joy to Mahaen, but the private void remained.

The Last Battle

"Lizard-skin." The taunt might have seemed comical if Ama's reaction had not been so severe. His screaming and shouting drew a crowd on both sides. Young men from Haenam opposed Ama's allies from Kamur. Spit flew, punches were thrown, and shoving degenerated into bruising wrestling as jeering and cheering escalated. Knives let the first blood and scattered the crowd at nightfall. The next day Haenam and Kamur men, young and old, brought out their lethal weapons. Volleys of arrows shrieked through the air, keeping opponents at some distance. Spears were brandished but reserved for the final battle after arrows were exhausted.

Most of the arrows arced high through the air, giving the target time to calibrate and dodge the trajectory. But one Haenam warrior, Toh, had spent weeks carving and stringing a new bow tighter than any before. He stepped back to avoid the arc of an approaching arrow, leveled his bow to aim directly at his enemy, and released his first arrow. As it whistled through the air, Toh was disappointed to see it falling below its mark. It impaled a Kamur warrior's foot, forcing him to the ground. Toh loaded his next arrow and considered adjusting his aim, but quickly realized that his target was now low to the ground. He leveled his bow precisely again, loosed his second arrow, and a second later it pierced that warrior's heart. The dying warrior's young wife unleashed a scream of agony as she raced through the fusillade of arrows toward his body. Having taken a life, the men of Haenam backed away from the firing line with bows still pointed at their enemies. The men of Kamur surrounded their fallen warrior with bows and spears ready, reluctantly acknowledging temporary defeat—but vowing they would bring the fight to Haenam another day.

Ancient Ritual

Tuan Don's reaction to this latest battle was different than in prior battles. He had pleaded with them before to abandon their violence. He had scolded and reasoned and had recruited Sawi leaders to negotiate peace. But this time, *Tuan* Don announced his decision to leave Kamur and search for a peaceful Sawi village in which to relocate his family.

As the old men of Kamur and Haenam separately discussed the implications of Don's decision, the young men cut new arrows and restrung their bows for the next fight. The consensus among the elders of each village was similar. There was no peaceful Sawi village where Don could settle. Tamor, Sato, Ero, and Hahami were trapped in the same endless cycle of revenge as Kamur, Haenam, Esep, and Wasohwi. Some said that effectively neutralized *Tuan* Don's threat, but others concluded that the pervasive violence would simply drive *Tuan* Don away from the Sawi permanently— along with the wealth and advantage they knew accompanied the presence of every foreigner. They did not want to waste the strategic opportunity Don represented.

That night Kani and Mahaen walked from the Haenam men's house, unarmed, toward the Kamur men's house. Hato, Kaiyo, and Kigo, also unarmed, met them on the moonlit path. Adrenaline threatened to cloud their judgment, but the heaviness in Mahaen's soul grounded him to the sober reality of the moment. He faced his peers with an ultimatum.

As Mahaen spoke, describing the only solution each of them knew would be effective, the adrenaline drained from all of them. Toned muscles shivered inadvertently in the cool night air. All of them knew the cost of battle. They had lost fathers, uncles, brothers, and cousins to hatchets, arrows, and spears. Some had even lost mothers, aunts, or sisters that ventured into the fray. But their minds and muscles were trained for battle. They were not trained for surrender. The path to peace was overgrown from disuse.

Hato shuddered as he recalled the time he had given his own child to the neighboring Kayagar tribe in a vain attempt to make peace. A Kayagar warrior had killed and eaten his son. Hato thought of his six remaining children and knew the price of securing peace was too high for him to consider paying.

Kigo and Kani were stoic—their minds reeling. Mahaen and Kaiyo locked their gazes on each other and silently made a pact.

The next morning was a tumult of confusion. The adults were playing out a drama that the children did not understand. First Mahaen walked from Haenam toward Kamur carrying one of his sons, only to have it wrestled from his arms by his wife. Then someone else set out from Kamur carrying his son—only to relent seconds later. It was like the pains of childbirth. Each contraction seemed destined to strangle those in its grip.

Then Kaiyo came forward holding his only son, Biakadon, and asked Mahor, a Haenam warrior, to advocate for peace with Kamur. Mahaen then returned with his youngest son, Mani, asking Kaiyo to advocate for peace with Haenam. The journey to peace began with these three men and two small boys. The tumult continued as hundreds of Sawi men, women, and children placed their hands on the 'peace children' signifying their acceptance of this exchange as a foundation for peace between Kamur and Haenam. In the celebration that followed, gifts were exchanged to demonstrate goodwill. The men of each village even exchanged names to signify their new kinship.

The battle of the previous day dissolved into peace and celebration on this new day. The adults, having known the pain of life and death without peace, sensed the uncertain promise of the new day.

But the Sawi children had no idea what had happened. They had no reference point to understand the significance of the 'peace child' exchange. It was just a day of peace in what would become, for them, a lifetime of peace.

4

COOL WATER

Early Childhood

His earliest memories are of his loving parents.

As an only child, Mani spent a lot of time with his mother, Wumi, as she tended to her daily routines. He learned to bail water steadily from their canoe as she stood paddling the Tumdu on their commute upriver into the surrounding forest. He sat by her side for hours as she tossed her fish-hook into the murky Kronkel River. He helped her forage for scarce tinder for their cooking fire. Abundant rain and constant humidity rendered most of the available wood unusable, but tree bark was a workable option. When Wumi felled a sago palm, Mani helped her scrape the spongy starch into a bowl to begin the magical transformation into their dietary staple. As the sun set, and the embers of the cooking fire faded, he often fell asleep on her warm lap.

Mani's father, Kaiyo, was highly respected in Kamur. His gentle spirit was in stark contrast to the volatile disposition of many of his peers. Mani saw that all the older men had deep scars, broken teeth, and contorted limbs. He sensed that behind their eyes were dark secrets beyond his understanding. When tempers flared, Kaiyo was often the voice of reason and reconciliation. He was an adept hunter. Fruit bats, snakes, swamp birds, and an occasional wild boar added variety and protein to their diet. His house was simple and sturdy. Mani loved to trek through the forest with the other boys trailing his father and uncles on their latest adventure. But the thin veneer of male camaraderie often splintered unpredictably, voices roared, muscles tensed, weapons were brandished. All of it scared Mani.

Beyond his family, Mani's world was defined by one other constant—water. In rainy season the shores of the Kronkel and Tumdu overflowed, transforming puddles into ponds and paths into streams. He waded barefoot through the village with his childhood friends searching for an abandoned canoe to train their balance and paddling skills. The riverbank provided a ready launching pad for reckless tumbling through the rain into the river. Peals of thunder resonated in Mani's bones, signaling the arrival or retreat of another downpour. An upturned face could easily provide his fill of cool water falling from precipitous heights. When the rain paused, the tropical sun boiled water from exposed leaves or skin to refresh its cycle. Water was omnipresent and ordinary. It was life.

Some of Mani's childhood friends had nicknames given by their peers, often describing their unique appearance or a notable public pratfall. Mani didn't have a nickname, but he sometimes overheard an adult whisper "cool water" to their companion as they pursed their lips in his direction.

While his peers included and excluded him according to the normal ebb and flow of childhood whims, adults seemed to always be watching and measuring his behavior. Day by day his carefree childhood became increasingly weighted by a vague but growing sense of responsibility. For what, he didn't know, but he would soon learn.

Learning Important Lessons

When the primary school opened in Kamur it was understood that Mani would attend. Some of his peers continued their aimless recreation, but Kaiyo and Wumi wanted him to focus his energy and attention on education. He proved to be an apt student with insatiable curiosity. He soon learned that he was also an able communicator. When his fellow students failed to grasp a new lesson, Mani described it in terms they could easily understand. Before long, his teachers were enlisting his assistance and mentoring him along the path toward a career in teaching.

One afternoon as he was wading home from primary school, Mani overheard an adult murmur "cool water" as he passed. The coincidence no longer seemed coincidental. So, that evening he asked his parents about the reference. That's when they told him the story of his adoption.

It was the first time Mani heard of the Sawi custom of exchanging children between warring clans to secure peace. He had lived his young life entirely at peace, but his father Kaiyo explained that the broken teeth and twisted limbs of the older men were from lifetimes spent in lethal battle. He told Mani the story of how through tears he had given his only son, Biakadon, to Mahor in order to make peace between Kamur and Haenam. He explained that this was the only way *Tuan* Don was convinced to stay in Kamur. Mani's birth father, Mahaen, had reciprocated by giving Mani to Kaiyo to make "cool water"—the Sawi term for peace. Kaiyo also explained that he had not told Mani about his adoption when he was younger because he was afraid he might run away to his birth parents and endanger the peace. Mani was shocked to learn he was adopted and unclear on the implications of being a peace child. He was stunned to hear that his classmate, Biakadon, was also a peace child. He was just beginning to understand that the sense of responsibility he felt was not something he merely imagined but was integral to the peace and harmony of the entire community.

Mani had known *Tuan* Don for as long as he could remember. *Tuan* Don's sons, Stephen and Shannon, were among his friends. He often saw *Tuan* Don around Kamur and at the Kalvari church. Mani loved listening to the stories *Tuan* Don told of Myao Kodon and his son Yesus. He had heard Yesus called "God's peace child."

The next day Kaiyo and Wumi told Mani they would travel with him to Haenam to meet his birth parents, Mahaen and Syado. It was a sweet reunion. Although Mani had no memory of his life with them, they dearly remembered their life with him—and the pain of sacrificing him to secure the peace. They had watched him grow up in neighboring Kamur but were careful not to risk the peace by revealing any hint of their shared heritage. Kaiyo's and Wumi's generous introduction opened the doors for Mahaen and Syado to publicly admit and demonstrate their love for Mani. For his part, Mani felt doubly blessed to have two sets of loving parents. He continued to live with Kaiyo and Wumi but always embraced Mahaen and Syado when their paths frequently crossed.

As Mani learned more about his place as a Sawi peace child, a deep yearning developed within him to know God's peace child. He accompanied his parents to Kalvari church at every opportunity. He listened intently to *Tuan* Don and to Pastor Amhwi as they taught from The Book about Myao Kodon. Mani increasingly sensed that Myao Kodon cared personally for him, was intentionally strengthening him, and was enabling him to carry the weight of responsibility he felt for preserving the peace within the Sawi community. It was as if God Himself had called Mani to this crucial role.

As all these truths converged in his life, he asked God's peace child, Yesus, to be his own Lord and Savior.

A few years later, Biakadon fell ill with malaria. Within a few days he succumbed to the fever. His death hit Mani hard. Although they had never spoken to one another about their peace child experiences, Mani felt like Biakadon shared the responsibility for keeping the peace. After Biakadon died, Mani felt the full weight of this responsibility. Peace felt precarious in the days immediately following Biakadon's death, and Mani flinched more than once when adult tempers flared. But peace had gained a foothold among the Sawi along with the gospel. By this time Netherlands New Guinea had also been ceded to the nation of Indonesia and government police officers were stationed in Kamur. The peace held.

Higher Education

After completing primary school in Kamur, Mani went to middle school and high school in the government center of Agats. This was his first experience traveling away from the Sawi villages and expanded his world both literally and figuratively. His interest in teaching continued to grow and was cultivated by his instructors. Mani was the first Sawi to complete high school.

He then traveled to Wamena, in the highlands of Papua, to attend teacher's training college. Mahaen and Syado sent money for his expenses. Mani soon earned a Bachelor of Arts degree in Education. After becoming a Christian, he adopted the name Yohannes (John), by which he is known today. By the time Yohannes returned to Kamur, *Tuan* Don had moved away. The combination of Don's departure and Yohannes' maturation resulted in a noticeable decrease in the community's expectations for him. Peace was increasingly assured by the presence of the Prince of Peace in Sawi hearts.

Professional Advancement

Indonesian teachers are civil servants. It was 1989 when Yohannes gained his first teaching position. In 2011 he was promoted to school superintendent. By 2017 he was appointed to the government position of District Supervisor. As the older generations of Sawi pass away, along with their memories of days past, Yohannes' educational and professional achievements have gradually eclipsed his reputation as a Sawi peace child.

In 2019, Yohannes is still a few years away from his retirement as a civil servant. His family lives in a modest house next to the hospital in Kamur. Two years ago, cellular phone service reached the Sawi. Last year Kamur began undertaking its first road project. Barges brought in gravel to raise the roadbed above the flood plain. A small concrete mixer extends the road one wheelbarrow at a time. The primary use of the road is as a clean footpath. One or two motorcycles have made their way by boat to Kamur but are ill-suited to the swampy terrain. When completed, the road will extend about a mile, from the Tumdu to the northern bend of the Kronkel. The next hope is for the government-owned utility company to install diesel generators for reliable electricity.

Yohannes' Legacy

Yohannes has spent his entire life at peace. He has heard the stories of revenge and betrayal, but they are from other lifetimes—not his own. Though he had no voice in his father's decision to make him a peace child, he accepted the responsibility as he came to understand his place in the community. He grew up hearing the gospel of Jesus Christ boldly proclaimed and made his own decision to turn from sin and follow Jesus as Lord and Savior.

He pursued education not only for personal and professional development but also for community development. By blazing the Sawi trail to higher education, he inaugurated a new era of learning for all Sawi. He was the first to complete college, but he was not the last. Dozens of young Sawi men and women have earned advanced degrees at Indonesian universities in Merauke, Timika, Wamena, Manokwari, Jayapura, and Jakarta. Yohannes' example of investing his life within the Sawi community has inspired many of these educated young people to do the same. Though the temptations of distant cities and opportunities call, they choose to return home to serve their people and build a better future for the Sawi and their neighbors.

THE SAWI NEW TESTAMENT

A Word of Caution

I n Bible college Don had been warned, "As you are learning the language and culture, you must be careful not to show respect for local traditional beliefs which may later prove to contradict Biblical teaching." As Don strained to capture each fleeting Sawi word, that lesson from Bible college reminded him that he was venturing into a theological minefield. Words that initially seemed harmless might later be discovered to have hidden meaning or symbolism. Phrases, sentences, and stories increased the complexity and the risk of confusion.

Cross-cultural missionaries are trained to be alert for any signs of developing syncretism, the merging of Christian doctrines with traditional religious beliefs, as they teach the local people. Christian teaching does not typically enter a local spiritual vacuum but arrives as a new spiritual perspective. As the local people consider the new perspective, they inevitably compare and contrast it to their traditional and contemporary beliefs. The danger in this is that what can develop from this confluence of ideas may more closely resemble their traditional animism and spiritism than biblical Christianity—especially where no Bible exists in the local language. Scripture in the local language creates a solid reference for understanding the differences between traditional religious beliefs and Christianity. As Paul said in 2 Timothy 3:16, "All Scripture is God-breathed and is useful for teaching, rebuking, correcting and training in righteousness."

In this light, Don ventured into the shadows of the Sawi language and culture, searching for clues that would help him accurately communicate the New Testament of God's truth.

Learning the Sawi Language

Don began slowly, pointing his finger at various objects to see how the Sawi would respond. Repeatedly, regardless of where he pointed, the Sawi answered precisely the same way—"*ririg*." Eventually Don learned this was the Sawi word for "finger" and that the Sawi instead pointed by thrusting their lips forward. This was the beginning of learning the Sawi language, but Don quickly ran out of nouns within lip range.

Linguistic training equips a person to discern the unique sounds of a language, create an alphabet to represent those sounds, progressively acquire vocabulary, and analyze the grammar in order to learn the language. For many languages this analytical process has taken foreigners ten to fifteen years to accomplish—before they attempt to translate Scripture into the language. One of the reasons language learning takes so much time is because acquiring a broad vocabulary normally requires experiencing a wide range of cultural events. Language describes life and death, history, the present, the future, and the hereafter. It describes physical, emotional, social, and spiritual dimensions. Life is the textbook for this education. But life takes a lifetime.

Unwilling simply to wait for vocabulary to surface slowly over a lifetime, Don devised a simple way to expand his vocabulary quickly. He noticed that many Sawi words contained similar patterns of consonants and vowels. So, each time he learned a new word he began asking whether there were other Sawi words that rhymed with it. For example, when he learned the Sawi word *ririg*, he could ask, "Do you ever say *girig*, *mirig*, or *wirig*?" Don described this as "Getting words to come to me, instead of waiting to find them by accident." Using this method, he learned thousands of Sawi words long before they would ever surface in conversation, allowing him to begin Bible translation much sooner. Decades later Don called his language-learning method "VAMP—Vocabulary Acquisition Made Practical."

Teaching Them to Obey All Things

Don enlisted the help of many Sawi to assist in translating the New Testament. Mavo, the first Sawi to put his faith in Jesus Christ, became a key translation assistant and early leader in the emerging Sawi church. Isai, the young boy who hid in the treetops when Don first arrived, also became an evangelist and translation assistant. Narai, the one who had signaled Don's return with Carol and Stephen by blowing a bamboo horn, helped Don learn the Sawi language, culture, and history. Amhwi, the second Sawi believer, drawn to Christ by watching Mavo, was also part of the translation team. Toh, the archer whose lethal arrows led to the peace child exchange, became another early believer, evangelist, church leader, and translation assistant.

When these five men came to faith in Christ, their first priority was spreading the good news of the gospel. But in an environment where most of their time was spent hunting and gathering resources from the surrounding forest, making time for evangelism impacted their very survival. Nevertheless, they sensed God's calling on them as Sawi leaders, and the urgency of the gospel message for their people. Don also saw these challenges and responded by providing the five evangelists with a modest financial stipend, as well as salt and noodles they could trade for staples as they traveled among more distant Sawi villages.

It was also clear to Don that discipleship had to follow and overlap with evangelism immediately. This meant two things. First, he had to make progress in translating the New Testament. Second, he would use the progressive Sawi Bible translation as the textbook for a Sawi Bible school. Rather than tackling these priorities sequentially, Don chose to address them simultaneously.

Within a few weeks, a half dozen Christian believers grew to a dozen. These twelve became the initial students in Don's Bible school, "Teaching them to obey everything I have commanded you" (Mt. 28:20). With existing Indonesian Bible translations, and English translations, as source texts, Don discussed the verses, passages, chapters, and books of the New Testament with these Sawi leaders. As they became grounded in the truths of Scripture, Don drafted and tested their understanding of the Sawi translation. Iron sharpened iron throughout this process.

Interwoven throughout the language learning and Bible translation, Don produced 19 progressive reading primers to teach the Sawi their alphabet and how to read Scripture. As with any innovation, some Sawi immediately grasped the principles and were able to apply them effectively while others struggled to conform their oral mindset to the constraints of writing.

The first Sawi church, built by the Sawi themselves, was in Kamur village and was readily accessible to the people in both Kamur and Haenam. As Don and the five evangelists traveled to other Sawi villages, more people began responding to the gospel. Within a few years, a second church was built in Seremeet and a third was built in Yohwi. During their first Christian decade the Sawi built churches in 15 villages.

Scripture Impact

During this same decade, the Sawi New Testament progressively came together. Every new verse, passage, chapter, and book expanded the conversation and deepened their spiritual understanding. Young believers grew in their knowledge of God's character and precepts. The Holy Spirit drew men, women, and children to faith in Christ. Scripture translation drafts were progressively refined and circulated within the community. Questions and feedback informed Don and his translation assistants as they revised their drafts. The result was a Bible translation that spoke Sawi.

God's voice was not merely informing the Sawi—it was transforming them. Peace gradually transplanted violence. Love pushed back hatred. Forgiveness replaced vengeance. It was not instantaneous. Instead, truth was planted in their hearts, godly character grew with time and opportunity, and the harvest of righteousness among the Sawi increased.

As the light of Scripture spread through the Sawi villages, it reached a point where even the most carefully hidden darkness was driven out. It began with an individual throwing away his amulets and occult fetishes. Then a second, and a third, person abandoned their charms and talismans to the same place. Soon, the discarded wood and rock carvings, bleached bones, feathers, and broken teeth swelled to a critical mass as the Holy Spirit displaced the evil spirits that had plagued the Sawi for generations. Consensus grew that the only appropriate end for these icons was to be consumed by fire. So, one evening after everyone had publicly discarded their private past, the Sawi elders set fire to them—and the previously hidden darkness was consumed by blazing Light. It was another mark of progress in the lengthening and strengthening Sawi journey of faith.

Missiology

At a time when many New Testament translations into tribal languages were requiring 20 to 30 years to complete, Don and his Sawi assistants completed the Sawi New Testament in 11 years. However, the isolation of his work among the Sawi limited broader awareness of Don's translation and evangelism strategies. That changed abruptly when *Peace Child* began circulating. Because of the prevailing missionary concerns regarding traditional beliefs, Don was occasionally criticized for linking the Sawi peace traditions with the Christian gospel. Some predicted the certain demise of the Sawi church because of this cultural connection. At a regional mission conference, one of Don's contemporaries publicly proclaimed, "The Sawi church will probably not last very long, because Don has involved so much of Sawi culture in the planting of the church." But those closest to Don saw the impact among the Sawi and respected him. He was elected as field leader and was invited regularly to speak at missionary gatherings to share what he'd learned.

In recalling his own journey of learning about what he would later call "redemptive analogies," Don remembered learning about the "new birth" ceremonies of another Papuan tribe. He asked the missionaries there, "Are you making use of their 'new birth' ceremony to explain biblical new birth?" Their initial answer was, "No. We don't want to confuse them." Their thinking was that if they found something in the culture that paralleled biblical truth, it was clear evidence that Satan was trying to distract the local people with deception to cement their misunderstanding of biblical truth. Over time more missionaries began testing redemptive analogies in their evangelism strategies.

As Don pondered these questions, Romans 2:14-15, a parenthetical statement by Paul within the broader context of his letter to the Roman Christians, seemed to provide the biblical answer.

"Indeed, when Gentiles, who do not have the law, do by nature things required by the law, they are a law for themselves, even though they do not have the law, since they show that the requirements of the law are written on their hearts, their consciences also bearing witness, and their thoughts now accusing, now even defending them."

As Don saw how God used the peace child analogy not only to draw the Sawi to Himself, but also to subsequently transform their lives, he rested on the assurance of these verses—seeing their reality unfold in the growth and health of the Sawi church.

During this same season of Christian missions, a missiologist named Don McGavran was advancing a theory called "people movements." The basic hypothesis was that most non-Western language groups in the world make decisions as a group rather than as individuals. In his books and teaching he cited many examples of people choosing to put their faith in Christ together. This in no way diminished the individual component of their decision. On the contrary, it illustrated that Christian conversion was not always a matter of sequential decisions but could be the result of parallel or simultaneous decisions. Don was, naturally, curious to see how these decisions would be made within the Sawi culture. In general, the decisions to put their faith in Christ proceeded along family lines. One person in the family would make his or her decision, and then others would follow. It was not a matter of one person deciding on behalf of everyone else. But the proximity and evidence of a life transformed by God naturally had its greatest impact within the family.

The Story Gets Out

In 1972, Don invited Rolf Forsberg and Gospel Films to come to Kamur to film the *Peace Child* story. Rolf narrated the story as Don, Carol, and the Sawi reenacted the history leading to the peace child exchange. The result was a 28-minute documentary that began circulating among American and Canadian churches, seminaries, and mission agencies, beginning in late 1973. It was a vivid reminder that even at that stage in modern history, people were still living in primitive isolation and practicing cannibalism. It was also a clarion call for Christian missionaries to focus on the frontiers, to reach the unreached, and to believe God for the outcome.

The following year (1974), the book *Peace Child* was published by Regal Books. In January 1976 the story was published by *Reader's Digest* as a condensed book. Based on their circulation at the time, *Reader's Digest* estimated that more than 100 million people worldwide read its *Peace Child* condensation. Tens, and eventually hundreds, of thousands of copies of *Peace Child* were purchased in the years following.

A Chapter Comes to a Close

After completing the Sawi New Testament, and establishing the Sawi church on that firm foundation, Don began looking toward new horizons to continue his work. Just northwest of the Sawi were the Auyu people. By the mid-1960s, missionary colleagues had begun pioneering work there, but they were struggling to learn the language. They learned of Don's unique language-learning approach and thought there might be similarities between the Auyu and Sawi languages. By the mid-1970s, they invited Don and Carol to consider joining their team.

Tearful Goodbyes

After almost 12 years living and working among the Sawi, it was difficult for the Richardson family to say goodbye. Deep personal friendships had been forged. The once-foreign language and culture had grown familiar. Blood, sweat, tears, and Christian faith knit all their hearts together. Carol had touched thousands of lives with medicine to heal gaping wounds and hidden diseases. Stephen, Shannon, and Paul Richardson had grown to be young men alongside their Sawi friends. Don's only daughter, Valerie, was just a toddler but had thrived in the familiar, nurturing community. Don had been the Sawi's pastor, mentor, and advocate. The seed of the gospel that God had planted in Sawi culture had grown to become the Sawi church. It would have been easy for the Richardsons to stay with the Sawi, but God had higher plans in mind for both the Richardsons and the Sawi.

As the Sawi grieved the Richardsons' imminent departure, Hato, the one-eyed Sawi leader, comforted the people by declaring they were sending Don as their peace child to the Auyu. The Richardsons assisted the missionaries to the Auyu with language learning for 18 months before departing for furlough in 1977.

6

GROWING IN FAITH

A New Calling

Within a short time after the release of the *Peace Child* film and book, Regions Beyond Missionary Union (now World Team), the Richardsons' mission sending agency, was inundated by requests for Don to speak at churches, colleges, and missions events. Don's organizational leaders appealed to him to accept a position as "Minister at Large" for the ministry. Although this was not part of Don's original vision, it was clear that God was moving in an unexpected way through the *Peace Child* story. Don accepted the position and joined Dr. Ralph Winter at the newly formed U.S. Center for World Mission in Pasadena, California as the Director of Tribal Peoples Studies.

Over the next 40 years Don spoke at thousands of gatherings to hundreds of thousands of people, challenging their presuppositions about tribal people and inspiring them to engage personally in missions through prayer, stewardship, and service. In 1977 he published *Lords of the Earth.* Four years later he published *Eternity in Their Hearts*, influencing the thinking of subsequent generations of Christian missionaries. His collaboration with Dr. Winter during these years eventually led to the creation of the Perspectives on the World Christian Movement course. These classes put the latest missiological thinking and strategies within reach of tens of thousands of Christians worldwide. Don ultimately spoke in all 50 states and 36 countries, so his lifetime of service in missions is widely known and highly respected.

A New Season for the Sawi

In 1973, John and Esther Mills had joined the Richardsons to minister to the Sawi. Naturally, in their early years, language learning was their priority. They also led literacy classes to teach the Sawi to read their own language. John worked alongside Don to merge with his ministry efforts. Esther worked alongside Carol to learn how to manage the medical clinic and treat the local illnesses. By the time the Richardsons departed, the Mills had a few years of experience working among the Sawi.

During the earliest years of the Sawi church, the five leaders—Mavo, Isai, Narai, Amhwi, and Toh—shouldered most of the responsibility for evangelism, preaching, and discipleship. From the outside, these men could have been described just as Peter and John were described in Acts 4:13. "They were unschooled, ordinary men." But the Sawi knew them as "men [who] had been with Jesus." Just as with Peter and John, no one could dispute the power of God at work in and through the lives of these men. Because of their testimonies and teaching, hundreds of Sawi put their faith in Jesus Christ. These men baptized thousands of new believers. Sawi churches spread throughout their communities. Bible studies and Christian education were anchored in the churches but also overflowed into their homes.

The Bible school that Don had started, with 12 students, was continued by John Mills after Don's departure. Together John and the Sawi leaders also began tackling translation of the Pentateuch, the first five books of the Old Testament.

Amhwi's Insight

As John and Amhwi sat together, discussing Genesis 34-37, Amhwi became quiet and wistful. He said, "I just realized that I am paddling in the same dugout canoe with the Patriarch Jacob." John was puzzled, so Amhwi explained.

Amhwi had experienced three severe tragedies in close succession within his immediate family. The normal assumption during these experiences is that evil spirits are angry and punishing the offenders. For a new Christian, this posed a great temptation to abandon his faith and return to occult spiritism. One of Amhwi's brothers suffered from epileptic seizures throughout his life. He had recently suffered a seizure while paddling alone in his canoe. He fell into the river and drowned. Another of his brothers had been catastrophically maimed when a policeman, wanting to demonstrate the deafening sound of his gun, accidentally shot him in the jaw. Then, one of Amhwi's children died from malarial fever.

"What does this have to do with Jacob?" John asked.

Amhwi responded, "Haven't you been paying attention to what we've been translating? Jacob experienced three personal tragedies in his life, but he didn't let them discourage his faith. He continued believing in God, and I am doing the same thing. Jacob and I are paddling in the same dugout canoe, coping with the same problems."

John continued, "But what were the three tragedies in Jacob's life?"

Amhwi reflected, "Jacob's daughter, Dinah, was raped by Shechem. His beloved wife, Rachel, died giving birth to Benjamin. Jacob's favorite son, Joseph, was missing and presumed dead."

Clearly God was giving the Sawi church leaders spiritual insight, feeding them from His Word, strengthening them as they led the church.

The Wisdom of Chickens

Another Sawi elder, Aidon, was asked to preach to the community about thankfulness for God's grace and mercy. He studied Scripture and, at Don's suggestion, prayed for God to give him an illustration that would provide spiritual insight and inspiration as he spoke to the congregation. As Aidon preached from Scripture, he carefully outlined the truths of God's grace and mercy, and the biblical exhortation for His children to be thankful. Then he gave his illustration.

"We should all recognize chickens as examples for us as believers."

The congregation sat in stunned silence. What in the world was the connection between chickens and thankfulness? They waited impatiently for his explanation.

"You might notice, if a chicken picks up so much as a sip of water in its beak, before it swallows—it lifts up its head and looks up to God. If a chicken picks up a seed, before it swallows the seed—the chicken looks up to God. Chickens are an example for us, demonstrating gratitude for every sip of water and for every seed they eat."

It was an illustration that no foreigner would ever imagine but that every Sawi understood clearly. "Yes! Let's remember the example of the chicken!" the crowd chanted in unison.

Church Discipline

For the Sawi, the Richardsons and Mills were invaluable teachers of God's truth. One of the marks of their quality as teachers is that they taught the Sawi to examine Scripture for themselves, and not to be dependent upon foreigners. As a result, the Sawi church leaders have always turned to God's Word for guidance in addressing threats to the church.

When a believer committed a sin, the community soon knew. Privacy was a scarce commodity among the Sawi. So, the elders were faced with the responsibility to address the sinner or be perceived as tacitly approving the sin. This followed naturally with the role of the village elders in maintaining cultural behavioral norms and was shaped by their study of Matthew 18, 1 Corinthians 5, and Hebrews 12. Their goal in confronting the sinner was repentance and restoration, motivated by love.

Typically, the pastor and elders would call the sinner to account for their actions privately, describing their actions as unworthy of a believer and not representative of what the church stands for. Often the sinner would repent immediately. But in cases where he or she would not, the elders would establish boundaries for their participation in church activities. Whether the offender was repentant or not, often the elders would ask the individual not to participate in the Lord's Supper for some weeks or months while reflecting on the gravity of the sin. In this way, the whole congregation also recognized the seriousness of sin. If the sin involved thievery or damage to someone's property, restitution was required before returning to the full fellowship of the church.

Selecting Pastors and Elders

As the gospel continued to transform more and more lives, it was natural for the early Sawi church leaders to begin appointing elders and deacons to share in teaching and caring for the growing flock. Because both Christian and secular education was still a new experience for the Sawi, there was no pool of seminary-trained pastoral candidates. So, the Sawi turned to Scripture for guidance in how to proceed. They turned to 1 and 2 Timothy and followed Paul's advice on identifying and selecting spiritual elders and deacons. This led them to confront their traditional practice of polygamy, as well as cultivating the godly character Paul describes as essential for Christian leaders.

Some of the men began evidencing a pastoral concern for others. As opportunities arose, they responded with comfort and counsel to their neighbors—believers and unbelievers alike. Over time, community consensus developed around those who were gifted as pastors and evidenced the fruit of the Holy Spirit in their lives. Those with community support found themselves with plenty of ministry opportunities. Those without community support found fewer and fewer opportunities.

Three collaborating mission organizations—Asia-Pacific Christian Mission (APCM), Regions Beyond Missionary Union (RBMU), and Unevangelized Fields Mission (UFM)—together formed the evangelical denomination known as Gospel Churches of Indonesia (Gereja Injili di Indonesia—GIDI) in 1973. Because of Don and Carol's affiliation with RBMU, the Sawi churches joined GIDI for fellowship and discipleship. So, from the earliest days of the Sawi church, they have been part of a growing body of Christians in Indonesia. They did not grow in isolation but in connection with the larger body of Christ—connected in their nation and connected to their spiritual brothers and sisters beyond their nation.

Practical Theology

As Don and I reflected on the establishment, growth, and strength of the Sawi church, he noted that many times local community leaders feel marginalized by the arrival of western missionaries. Their place of influence in the community is often unintentionally compromised by the interest in the missionary's new teachings, different ways of doing things, and technology. Don observed this during his time with the Sawi.

On the day of Don's first arrival in Kamur, the elders were the ones who determined the response of the Sawi people. It was their decision whether, or how, to respond to Don's intrusion into their community. They were the ones who welcomed Don and Carol with fear and trembling. But very quickly it became the younger Sawi men who found new opportunities for work with Don. Don hired young men to cut trees, drive the pilings for the foundation of his house, and work alongside him to finish the living space and thatch the roof.

In time, Don sensed the growing distance of the elders, and he determined to draw them closer and affirm their leadership in the community.

One night some young men attempted to break into Don's storage closet to steal from his supply of machetes, steel axes, knives, fishing line, fishhooks, and salt. Don awoke when he heard the floorboards creak, and he scared the men away in the darkness. Don saw the direction the would-be thieves had fled, and his first thought was to march down the path, wake up the village elders, and rant over their lack of appreciation for the sacrifices the Richardsons had made to live with them.

But immediately, the Holy Spirit whispered, "Don, you have been feeling concerned over the fact that most of the jobs you offer, most of the work that you need Sawi men to help with, is being given to young men. The older men are busy. They have families to care for. They have pigs to hunt and firewood to chop. So, most of the money you pay for help goes into the hands of the young men. The elders are being left on the sidelines, getting nothing because they are not available for you to call on at a moment's notice like all the young men who hang around your house all day hoping to get jobs. You have been asking Me for opportunity to affirm the elders' important role. Don't you see? This situation will give you a chance not only to deal with the stealing threat, but also to let the elders know that they are important to you."

So, the Holy Spirit guided Don down the village path to enlist the elders' help. He called them out of the men's houses by name. "Please. We need to talk." One by one they descended the long ladders and surrounded him. *"Tuan* Don, what's the problem? What's the matter?" Don led them back up the path to his house, showed them the intruders' wet footprints on the porch, and asked for their help in responding to the incident. "You are the elders of Kamur village. You are men of authority, whom the young men respect. Can I ask you to handle this problem? Will you announce that this must never happen again, and put fear into the hearts of those three young men (and everyone else)?"

In their eyes, Don was a millionaire. He had wealth beyond their imagination. With the goods in his storage closet, Don could have purchased perhaps 60 wives. With the push of a button on the radio, Don could talk to people hundreds of miles away and summon an airplane to land on the river with even more supplies. But this millionaire was asking for their help. He was admitting his vulnerability as an outsider and asking for their help as insiders. They knew he was honoring them by trusting their authority and influence in the community. "Don, you have asked for our help—and you've got it."

The elders turned on their heels, made their way back to the village, and took turns loudly lecturing everyone at the top of their lungs about the evils of stealing. The would-be thieves did not confess and were never identified. But there were no more threats of stealing. The word was out. If you try to steal from *Tuan* Don, the elders will come after you!

Over the years Don enlisted the elders to manage major construction projects on his behalf. They supervised clearing a thousand trees to make space for an airstrip. Later they oversaw the digging of a canal over a mile long to connect two rivers so that Don and the other evangelists could more easily reach the outlying Sawi villages.

Reflecting With Don

During our conversations, I sometimes wondered whether Don felt he had done the right thing by leaving the Sawi and responding to God's calling to reshape global missions thinking and strategy. I knew that he loved and missed the Sawi dearly.

As I listened to Don describe how he had personally mentored the first Sawi church leaders, and then within just a few years departed, an unexpected insight struck me.

I was thinking about how the Apostle Paul had traveled throughout the Mediterranean region proclaiming the gospel, planting churches, choosing elders, mentoring them—and leaving. As best we can tell from the Scriptural accounts, Paul never spent more than two or three years in any single place.

I said to Don, "As important as your arrival was to the Sawi people, your departure may have been even more important." Don's eyes became misty.

In my own four decades in international missions, I have seen many instances where foreign missionaries moved into the village for life. In too many of those cases, stunted growth of the local church resulted. As long as the missionary is present, he or she is the default leader, the recognized expert—held, appropriately, in high regard. But unless the missionaries intentionally affirm the local leaders, the church often remains dependent on outside authority.

The Sawi church leaders today are neither dependent nor independent. Instead, they are inter-dependent. They are part of the GIDI denominational leadership, linked to churches throughout Papua, Indonesia and beyond. They are not amputated, separated, from the global body of Christ. They are all as Paul described:

> "Baptized by one Spirit into one body—whether Jews or Greeks, slave or free—and we were all given the one Spirit to drink. ...In fact, God has arranged the parts in the body, every one of them [including the Sawi], just as He wanted them to be. ...God has given greater honor to the parts that lacked it, so that there would be no division in the body, but that its parts should have equal concern for each other."
> (1 Cor 12:13, 18, 24-25)

All of this, even Don's departure, prepared the Sawi church for the next season of their growth and ministry impact on their tribal neighbors—and the world.

7

Decades Pass

Economic Lessons

D on's vision for teaching the Sawi extended well beyond
Scripture. When the Richardsons arrived in Kamur,
Sawi houses were suspended above the flood plain within
the canopy of trees. When Don built the first home for himself and his family, he showed the Sawi how to drive pilings
into the swampy ground and create a level floor structure
just a few feet above the high-water level. Soon this innovation was being duplicated by the Sawi as they built their
own homes.

Later, when John and Esther Mills arrived, John taught the Sawi how to saw boards from logs by hand using a technique called pit-sawing. After digging a pit into the ground, a log would be rolled into position straddling the pit. Using a straight saw with two handles, one workman stands on top of the log while the other works from underneath the log, progressively sawing the log into boards lengthwise. The advantages of construction using boards and nails quickly led to its adoption for homes and church buildings.

As Don traveled in rural Papua, he noticed that Chinese entrepreneurs were seizing every opportunity to open stores to sell and trade goods with the local Papuans. Unfortunately, illiterate people like the Sawi were susceptible to being taken advantage by the savvy merchants. The local Sawi economy was based on self-sustaining hunting and gathering in the local rainforest, with occasional barter exchanges among consenting traders. Money only entered their economy when outsiders arrived. Different monetary values, and the importance of zeroes, were not intuitively obvious to the Sawi. So, Don taught them how to count money and compare the value to the trade goods.

Beyond teaching theory, Don trained several Sawi in the basics of retail management. Don became their wholesale supplier. He purchased various trade goods in sufficient quantities to get better prices, recruited interested Sawi to set up shops, divided the products among them, and helped them start their businesses. They decided to position the stores close together, and close to town, to discourage stealing. If anyone tried to break into a store overnight, the sound could be heard by those close by.

Very quickly, an unanticipated cultural problem surfaced. Among the Sawi, if a younger man has something valuable, an older relative has the right to claim it—and the younger person cannot withhold the item from the elder. As soon as this surfaced Don prayed for, and found, a workable solution. Each of the young Sawi entrepreneurs had older male relatives. Don encouraged each store owner to ask one older relative to become his "shield." "If an elder of my clan comes and sees something on my shelf that he wants, instead of just refusing his request impolitely, I will say that we must first talk to you—my shield. If you say I must give it to him, I will. But if you say no, he must accept your answer." In this way the elders of each family helped to guarantee the success of the younger men. It didn't take long for everyone to recognize the value of protecting the store's sustainability, because whenever the stock ran low they had to buy more, at wholesale cost, from Don.

Helping them launch businesses also created an opportunity for Don to teach them about tithing. Each time the store owners came to Don to purchase more products wholesale, Don asked them, "How much are you going to set aside as a contribution to the church?" Before making their purchase, they would make their decision about giving to the church. This became a natural part of their routine.

As the shops in Kamur began to enjoy some success, the Sawi believers began using stores to establish Christian families in other unchurched Sawi villages. By bringing value to the other communities, these Christian entrepreneurs led the way and increased the credibility of the Sawi evangelists.

Over the decades, the Sawi have fully transitioned from a barter system to a cash economy. Local civil service jobs have multiplied. It is increasingly common for young Sawi men to get work outside the local community and bring cash back for their families. Offerings to support the churches are typically made in cash today.

Along the way they also learned some harsh economic lessons. Before Don departed, he recruited a local Indonesian school teacher to take his place as the wholesale distributor for the Sawi retail stores. Unfortunately, the temptation of managing the cash soon got the better of this teacher, and he absconded with all the Sawi's money. The Sawi shop owners had to rebuild their businesses with only what money the families could gather. But this taught the families to protect their investments directly instead of depending upon someone else.

Education Increases

Don described the Indonesian government "following the footprints of the gospel." Early government outposts in the remote reaches of Netherland New Guinea were mostly defenseless against thieves and vandals. Government administrators, wearied of losing these battles with the locals, searched earnestly for people of peace and good will. Their searching inevitably led them to places where the gospel was transforming sinners' lives—places like Kamur.

Government education followed government administration. Primary schools formed to meet the early education needs of children. Because there was no history of local education, the first teachers came in from outside the Sawi communities—and taught in Indonesian. When Don arrived, Hadi became his interpreter because of his unique knowledge of three local languages. With the arrival of Indonesian education, nearly everyone in the next generation of Sawi became bilingual. While primary school was local, high schools and universities were regional. So, as Sawi students continued into higher education, they increasingly encountered people speaking even more languages. Bilingualism became the minimum requirement, and multilingualism became more common.

Publishing the Sawi New Testament

The copyright page of the Sawi New Testament shows it was published by the Indonesian Bible Society in 1994—21 years after Don and his Sawi assistants completed the translation.

When I first heard this date, I assumed it had to be an error. Perhaps this was simply a second or third printing under the authority of the Bible Society. Or, perhaps it was simply a misprint of the actual date. But as I talked with the Sawi, I realized it was not an error. It was the painful truth.

Only two of Don's original translation assistants are still alive: Mavo and Amhwi. Scripture portions were printed as they were translated. But when asked why it took two decades for the complete Sawi New Testament to be printed—they had no answer. It is a complete mystery to them. Printing was a decision and technology controlled by others. Foreigners made the decision, so only they know why the printing was delayed.

When the Richardsons moved from the Sawi to the Auyu in 1975, their missionary successors, John and Esther Mills, assumed primary responsibility for the ongoing work among the Sawi. Several priorities occupied the years that followed.

Although the Mills family initially overlapped with the Richardsons, benefitting from their knowledge of Sawi language and culture, John Mills invested in ongoing linguistic and anthropological analyses in order to strengthen their understanding of the Sawi. This led them in two directions.

First, it led them to increasing emphasis on literacy training for the Sawi. Literacy was viewed as an essential element of civilization, the foundation for both biblical and secular education, economic development, political participation, and social welfare. Without a solid foundation of literacy among the Sawi people, the Sawi New Testament would have few readers. At that point, audio Scriptures were often seen as compromising the priority of literacy as an overarching goal.

Second, it led John to revise the New Testament translation Don had done. As you might imagine, this was a sensitive issue between the two translators. It also created some confusion among the Sawi people as they compared and contrasted the variations in the translations. For their part, the Sawi church leaders did their best to answer the questions raised by both Don and John during the translation but always understood that the final translation decisions were made by the missionaries. The Sawi were the beneficiaries of the Scripture translation, and the missionaries were the benefactors.

The final publishing decision, and decision on copyright ownership, was neither shared with nor understood by the Sawi. They celebrated the publication of their New Testament and looked forward to the translation of the Old Testament. Their anticipation of the Old Testament would ultimately require another 24 years.

John Mills had begun translating the Pentateuch in the 1980s but did not finish. Over the years, his organizational and regional responsibilities increased and his local focus on the Sawi decreased. So, the Sawi church leaders carried on—leading the Sawi church.

Lack of Vision

Intermittently over the years, Don made return visits to Kamur. On one of these trips it seemed to him that the Sawi's interest in Scripture was waning. He began wondering whether the novelty had worn off, and complacency was beginning to take root. Brief conversations revealed that even many of the elders were not staying diligent in reading the Scriptures. For a moment, discouragement reared its ugly head. But soon Don realized the real root of the problem. The Sawi elders were gradually losing their eyesight—just as Don was! The light wasn't going out in their hearts; it was getting dimmer in their eyes!

When Don returned to the U.S., he mentioned this during a prayer meeting. "Can you pray that God will provide the funds or that I'll figure out a way to get eyeglasses back to the Sawi?" A brief shopping expedition suggested that reading glasses would be at least $6.00 apiece, which seemed out of reach financially for Don. A lady at the prayer meeting responded, "We don't need to pray about that. We can get them for $1.00 apiece at a local dollar store." So, an $1800 problem was reduced to $300, and Don brought 300 pairs of eyeglasses back to Kamur on his next visit.

Islam Reaches Kamur

Transmigration, which originally began as a Dutch colonial policy to reduce overpopulation on the island of Java, was continued by the Indonesian government throughout the late 20th and early 21st centuries. During these decades as many as 20 million Javanese were relocated to Kalimantan, Sumatra, and Papua. The cumulative impact in Papua is that the migrant Javanese Muslim population now exceeds the indigenous Papuan population. This has resulted in land disputes, political turmoil, and religious clashes.

The first Muslims arriving in Kamur were government administrators assigned to the remote outpost. Muslim policemen and school teachers followed. As they settled into the community, they naturally wanted a mosque for prayer and Islamic observances. Initially this created no concern for Sawi Christians, who saw it as a benign accommodation to the Muslim visitors in their community. But over time, one mosque became two, and their influence in the community began to increase. The Sawi church elders understood the Muslim threat to the Christian church and prayed for wisdom in how to respond.

In the meantime, Islam had become an increasing concern for Don. The terrorist attack on September 11, 2001 galvanized Don's commitment to speak against the rising threat of Islam. After extensive research, in 2003 he published *Secrets of the Koran*—an in-depth exposé of militant Koranic teachings for those without prior knowledge of its content.

Fiftieth Anniversary Reunion

In 2012 Don and his sons, Stephen, Shannon, and Paul, returned to Kamur to celebrate the 50th anniversary of their family's arrival there in 1962. The Sawi spent months preparing for this historic celebration.

A Mission Aviation Fellowship float plane delivered them to the Kronkel River, where they then stepped into a canoe manned by three of the original Kayagar paddlers and three daughters of the other deceased paddlers who had brought the Richardsons to Kamur 50 years before. The riverbanks were lined with thousands of Sawi, Asmat, Auyu, Kayagar, and Atohwaem Christians—Don's spiritual children, grand-children, and even great-grandchildren!

As part of the celebration, the church leaders invited any believers requesting baptism to come forward for instruction and exhortation before a group baptism. Don had been told to anticipate around fifty new believers for baptism in the Tumdu River. As the crowd listened to Don and the Sawi pastors' pre-baptism exhortations, the Holy Spirit moved another 265 unbaptized believers to step forward for baptism! Twenty-five at a time stepped into the water and were baptized by Don and the Sawi pastors! After the baptisms, everyone gathered at the church for additional teaching and discipleship.

In addition to the crowded Sunday church service, a marriage ceremony wed 102 couples, many of whom had been married for years by a tribal custom but wanted a Christian wedding and Indonesian marriage certificate. Following the mass wedding around 130 babies were dedicated to God. The entire visit was a testimony and celebration of God's power at work in and through the Sawi people for His glory.

Guarding Theological Truth

During the reunion in Kamur, Don met with Sawi church leaders to discuss the challenges to sound Christian doctrine they were facing within the churches. Multiple threats had surfaced in the years since Don had departed.

Cargo cult theology was an unanticipated byproduct of the contact of traditional and modern societies. Traditional people had never before seen manufactured goods. They knew everything about their natural environment, but the "cargo" that foreigners had was completely unknown to them. The conclusion reached by some tribes was that these things must have been created by deities. Fortunately, the Sawi learned from Don that this was not the case. But rumors among neighboring tribes occasionally fascinated vulnerable Sawi. The Sawi elders were careful to warn the people of these temptations.

Prosperity theology also made its way to Kamur. One preacher present during the 50th anniversary celebration was dressed head to toe in a white suit and told the people that if they followed God they would become wealthy. Apparently, Benny Hinn held a large gathering in the nearby city of Merauke, and by following his example this preacher was promising health and wealth to anyone who would follow Christ.

Over the years, Islam became an increasingly imposing threat to the Sawi church. The neighborhoods surrounding the mosques were reserved for Muslims. When Don asked the Sawi church leaders about the encroachment of Islam, he was assured. "We know about these things already." In fact, not long after the second mosque was built in Kamur, the Sawi leaders required that it be torn down. Their reasoning went like this: "This is our village. We are Christians. It is okay for outsiders to have a mosque for themselves, but we don't need mosques for the Sawi. One is enough." So, the second mosque was removed.

Whenever the Sawi encounter new religious teaching or philosophy, they respond by searching the Scriptures. They have a stable reference point in the New Testament. They are like the Bereans in Acts 17. They are not swayed by popular teachers or promises. They look to God's Word for guidance. They feed themselves spiritually from His Word and so stand strong against Satan's deceptions. God's Word is the sure foundation of their faith.

Still Speaking Sawi

One of the surprising realizations Steve Richardson had during the 50th anniversary reunion was how much the Sawi language was still being spoken in the villages. After all those years, Steve's Sawi had naturally languished. Given the passing years, and the impact of Indonesian being commonly spoken across minority language lines, he expected that Indonesian would be more common than the Sawi language in Kamur. That was definitely not the case.

Steve was more comfortable speaking in Indonesian, so he addressed the groups or individuals primarily using that language. But as he listened in on their conversations, he realized that the Sawi language was still preferred and widely used by the people. He was encouraged that he was able to still understand the Sawi language, but nonetheless found it easier to express himself in Indonesian. For the Sawi, it was exactly the opposite. They could understand the Indonesian language but preferred to express themselves using the Sawi language.

One reflection of the increasing bilingualism is that there are now separate church services conducted for Indonesian and Sawi languages.

Healthy Churches

In 1962, the Sawi were cannibals. In 2019, three out of four Sawi are second- and third-generation Christians. They are living examples of what Eugene Peterson called "a long obedience in the same direction."

Through Don's teaching and mentoring, early Sawi believers became pastors and evangelists. Together they carried the good news of the gospel to every Sawi village and family, planting the seeds of the Sawi church. Over the years these seeds, watered by thousands of baptisms, grew into 15 Sawi churches and spread beyond their boundaries to plant churches among their former enemies—the Asmat, Auyu,

Atohwaem, and Kayagar. The testimony of the faithfulness of Sawi believers spread throughout Papua, across Indonesia, and even to the United States and Canada—encouraging the faith of millions. They knit themselves into the fabric and fellowship of Christian churches across their nation and around the world.

God is Still Moving

But today, the memory of God's work among the Sawi is fading in the hearts and minds of those beyond the Sawi's horizon. The Sawi are out of sight and, therefore, out of mind. Except for another unexpected turn of events, the Sawi might easily have been forgotten. But God had something else in mind.

8

Don's Later Years

Unretiring

W hen I met Don, he was 70 years old. He jogged regularly. In fact, he competed in regional track meets where, on a few occasions, he took first place in his age-group. He was hiking to the summits of as many mountains over 14,000 feet in elevation as possible, ultimately summitting 33 of these peaks before a foot injury at age 79 put an end to that summertime hobby. He played tournament quality chess. He owned rental property. He painted scenes on canvas of tribal life from his missionary experiences. He wrote books, sold them online, and filled orders from his garage. He regularly traveled and spoke as part of the Perspectives on the World Christian Movement course. He spoke in churches and college mission conferences.

But between the invitations, I saw another sobering reality that I had seen in other missionaries' lives. Missionaries are most often financially supported by the generations older than them. By the time a missionary reaches retirement age, many of their supporters have died. In addition, missionaries' retirement benefits are typically significantly below those of their business peers. So, while Don was truly a 'renaissance man' with many talents, he was also an entrepreneur funding his ministry.

Another difficult reality of this season of life was that Don's *Peace Child* fame was aging along with him. Breaking news from the 1960s didn't have the same impact 50 years later. Even the boundaries of Christian missions had moved. Frontier tribal mission work of the mid-20th century was succeeded by the "10/40 Window" strategy in the 1990s and "AD 2000" strategies as the 20th century drew to a close.

As soon as we at Wycliffe Associates realized that Don Richardson was in our neighborhood, we began inviting him to speak about Bible translation at our events. He was a keynote speaker at several of our annual Summit events, as well as traveling thousands of miles on our seasonal banquet tours in dozens of communities across the U.S. During these years he built strong friendships with many members of our ministry team and encouraged thousands of our ministry partners in their support for Bible translation.

A New Bible Translation Strategy

When Don translated the Sawi New Testament, he was a foreign translator (not a native Sawi speaker) implementing a foreign-missions strategy. For frontier missionaries, working among non-Christian people, this was the only option for advancing Bible translation: <u>foreign translators</u> working under <u>foreign control</u>.

By the late 20th century, many of the mid-century missions strategies were bearing significant fruit. People worldwide had turned to Christ. Churches were planted and growing. This did not go unnoticed within Bible translation circles. During the 1980s and 1990s, several new organizations formed with the strategy of recruiting indigenous speakers of the language to carry an increasing responsibility for translating Scripture into their own languages. This strategy improved translation quality and accelerated the pace of Bible translation because the local speakers did not require a decade or more to learn the language and culture, and they understood the language nuances intuitively. This has been described as: <u>local translators</u> working under <u>foreign control</u>.

Through a series of God-ordained circumstances, in 2014 a new strategy for Bible translation emerged unexpectedly when a small group of Christians in South Asia decided they were unwilling to wait any longer for foreigners to translate Scripture into their language—they decided to do it themselves. Wycliffe Associates served them by providing translation training and technical tools, but all the decisions regarding the translation were made by the local Christians. This has been described as: <u>local translators</u> working under <u>local control</u>.

Wycliffe Associates called this strategy MAST—Mobilized Assistance Supporting Translation. As Don worked in close collaboration with our team, he gradually began hearing about how MAST was changing Bible translation around the world. What started with a single language spread to over a hundred languages within a year, and to more than a thousand languages within four years. Churches around the world were increasingly exercising their authority and responsibility as stewards of God's Word in their own languages. What was once impossible was actually happening!

Don's response to the emergence of MAST was excitement. "Making use of local Christians who are already bilingual and can use existing translations in their second language as a reference, is wise... and efficient. The locals know all the ins and outs of their language and culture that foreigners often struggle to learn. They understand the local idioms." We talked specifically about whether people who are bilingual need Scripture in their first language. Don reflected, "If one translation is good, two translations that confirm each other are even better. What is unclear to them in their second language may become clear to them in their first." As the impact of MAST grew and spread, Don was a constant encouragement to our team.

Unexpected Diagnosis

After experiencing symptoms of dizziness, fatigue, and spatial disorientation, in March 2018 Don underwent testing to explore the possible cause. An MRI provided the definitive diagnosis—he had a large mass in his brain. He was immediately scheduled for surgery to determine the nature of the mass, remove as much as possible, and clarify the treatment plan going forward. He weathered the exploratory surgery that removed the tumor, but the pathology report diagnosed the mass as glioblastoma multiforme, a very aggressive form of brain cancer. The prognosis was not optimistic so the medical team prescribed radiation treatments and chemotherapy for the coming months. Don initially tried to attack the cancer via nutritional and other alternative regimens. When a subsequent MRI showed the cancer growing back, he eventually submitted to doctors' recommendations. After a couple rounds of treatments, and weighing the impact on his quality of life, Don decided to discontinue the treatments.

His traveling days were over as he faced this new challenge. As word of Don's diagnosis spread through churches and the missions community worldwide, people were naturally quite shocked. Don was a missionary statesman, a patriarch and standard that thousands looked to for wisdom and inspiration. Although we all knew Don was mortal, the prospect of his final days came too soon.

Honoring Don's Legacy

It was fitting that mission leaders and organizations wanted to honor God for the work He had done in and through Don's life—while Don was still alive to praise God himself. Though the finish line was more visible, the pace and timing were not. So, recognitions and accolades followed soon after his recovery from surgery.

In June 2018 I was sitting in the audience, watching an award ceremony unfold. Don was being honored with a *Lifetime of Service* award. The presenter described Don's impact on Christian missions at length in appropriate superlatives. I wondered—how do you honor and recognize a lifetime of influence on thousands of missionaries impacting hundreds of millions of people worldwide? The presenter handed Don a plaque. My heart sank.

As Don took the podium and reflected on his lifetime in missions, I soaked in every word. I knew I was listening to a missionary statesman. During Don's address, I leaned over to whisper to my friend and colleague Brent Ropp, "There must be a better way to honor Don's lifetime of work." That got Brent thinking.

When the ceremony ended a few minutes later, Don was immediately surrounded by the crowd. As Brent and I drifted toward the hallway he said, "What if we help the Sawi finish the translation of their Bible? That would be a more appropriate honor than giving Don a plaque."

As soon as I heard Brent's question, several thoughts converged in my brain. First, over the 33 years Brent and I had known each other, this kind of interaction had happened hundreds of times—often leading to unprecedented and unimagined breakthroughs in ministry. I knew from experience that God was speaking through Brent. Second, because Don had spent his lifetime working to advance the gospel and Bible translation in every language, I knew this would be a fitting tribute and encouragement to him. Third, without knowing how much time Don would have on earth, the only way this could happen with his knowledge would be for the Sawi to mobilize a large number of bilingual translators within a short period of time. Fourth, I knew that only God could make it happen.

9

Providential Appointments

Yanti

Papuan Entrepreneurs

With hundreds of minority languages still without Scripture, the nation of Indonesia has long been a strategic priority for Bible translation. But the history of

Bible translation there has been difficult. Foreign mission organizations have gone through cycles of favor and disfavor with the government, some even being expelled from the country. Local Bible translation organizations have struggled due to limited resources. The net result is that today there are still hundreds of languages throughout Indonesia without a single verse of Scripture.

Papuan Indonesian Christians have observed the comings and goings of outsiders on their island their entire lives. Everyone seems to have a plan for them, often designed to leverage local resources for the benefit of outsiders, but few have asked them about their own vision for their own land and people. Some have, wrongly, assumed there is no local vision. But if you ask the Papuans, they describe very clear visions and goals for their people—and their plans to accomplish them.

Transportation within Papua is difficult. The island is mountainous, with the highest peaks reaching above 16,000 feet in elevation and mountain ranges extending hundreds of miles. Dense rainforest reaches from the coasts to the tree line above 12,000 feet. Tropical storms flood the slopes, creating frequent landslides. Foreigners initially overcame these challenges using airplanes. Building an airstrip, although very difficult in this terrain, required less time and expense than cutting roads and building bridges. Foreign contractors eventually came with heavy equipment to fulfill government contracts to build roads. Papuans saw foreign companies enriched by building their transportation infrastructure and taking advantage of local workers and communities in the process. So, they began competing for these contracts to benefit the local people.

In 2005 a young Papuan woman, Yanti, formed a Papuan road construction company using her network of local contacts. She soon found that her local knowledge of Papua gave her a solid advantage in competing against outside contractors. As the company continued to expand, tragically Yanti's husband died in a car accident. Since 2009 Yanti has managed the construction company on her own. But as she saw the roads extending further into her homeland, she came to a sobering realization. Roads were not transforming the Papuan people. Often the primary road users were outsiders exploiting the local people and resources.

Networking

In search of new ways to help Papuan people, Yanti joined the Papuan Transformation Community, a group of local business owners who were encouraging young Papuan entrepreneurs to create new businesses. There Yanti crossed paths with a couple aspiring young Papuan students. Christov was just beginning to study accounting at the university. Wesly was working in business and had studied English in preparation for an advanced business program in Australia. At the time, there was no hint of what God was preparing all of them to do for the people of Papua.

Several years passed. Christov finished his university studies and took a job on the island of Java as a forensic accountant. After some time in this position, he sensed God moving him in a new direction. In the summer of 2016, a friend encouraged Christov to apply for a position with an Indonesian company that had recently been formed to translate Christian materials into Indonesian languages. That company was Wycliffe Associates' local partner for supporting Bible translation in Indonesian languages. Although Christov knew nothing about Bible translation and felt he was too young to lead and manage this enterprise, at the age of 25 Christov became the general manager of this company.

The learning curve for Christov was steep. The MAST translation strategy was being used to assist Indonesian churches in launching Bible translations in new languages. Christov attended several MAST workshops to see it firsthand and learn how it worked. The company he managed provided computer tablets or laptops loaded with translation software and reference materials for the translators. The company also translated those references from English into Indonesian. Since he had grown up in Papua, he was aware that Bible translation often took foreigners decades to accomplish, but he saw miraculous progress as Indonesians accomplished Bible translation using MAST. In his words, "I soon realized that I was in the midst of the greatest change in Bible translation history." In his prior business experience, he had been confident in his own capabilities. But as he faced the challenges and opportunities of advancing Bible translation in Indonesia, he knew he was completely dependent upon God.

Within his first two years working with our partner company, Christov saw 150 Indonesian languages begin Bible translation.

Building the Team

Since most of the reference and training materials for Bible translation were created in English, at Wycliffe Associates we were intent on translating these into Indonesian so they could be readily accessible to Indonesian speakers. Finding Indonesians with a thorough knowledge of English was essential to make this vision a reality.

Sierra grew up in Sulawesi, the granddaughter of an Indonesian English teacher. Her grandmother had a university degree in English and took every opportunity to teach Sierra English from a very young age. In fact, Sierra grew up speaking "just four" languages. In college she majored in French and earned a Bachelor's degree in Education. Sierra joined the team initially to translate the English Bible translation references into Indonesian. But soon her teaching skills found an outlet as a facilitator for the MAST Bible translation workshops.

With new translation work spreading throughout the western Indonesian provinces, Christov naturally wanted to see Bible translation progress in his home province of Papua. In early 2017 he invited his Papuan business mentor, Yanti, to join the team. She agreed to become the Papua program manager responsible to lead and expand Bible translation throughout her Indonesian province. The government, business, and community contacts she had developed over the years managing the road construction business could be tremendously valuable in support of Bible translation.

To clear the path for future progress, it would be necessary to translate the Bible translation reference materials into Papuan Malay—the language of wider communication unique to Papua. In God's providence, Wesly's father, a Papuan pastor, joined the Papuan Malay translation team. By then Wesly had earned a Graduate Certificate in Business Administration and was pursuing business interests. But he was slowly beginning to realize that business was not satisfying the desire of his heart to see Papua transformed spiritually.

In the fall of 2017 Yanti assisted in facilitating a MAST workshop for three languages in her home area of Sentani. She immediately and enthusiastically agreed to host the event in her own home and recruit her friends and neighbors to participate in the translation event. Twenty-four women were among those who responded to her invitation to begin these Bible translations!

Mixed Emotions

With Don Richardson's encouragement, Brent Ropp and I began expanding the conversation within our Wycliffe Associates team about contacting the Sawi to gauge their interest in translating the Old Testament. As we explored the linguistic documentation of Sawi we found research classifying it as a dead language—no longer actively in use. This obviously contradicted what we'd heard from Don and Steve from their visit just a few years previous. The only way to know for sure would be to ask the Sawi. Brent opened the discussion with our Pacific Area team and asked them to make contact. The request soon reached Christov, who then asked Yanti to take the lead in reaching out to the Sawi church leaders.

As word of this potential translation effort spread among our Indonesian team, excitement and apprehension began building. The *Peace Child* story is widely known throughout Indonesia. Both the book and the film were translated into Indonesian and have had a wide audience. Christov, Sierra, and Yanti, and their extended families, knew of the Sawi's reputation. The opportunity to connect with the people whose repentance and faith was pivotal in Papuan history was exhilarating. At the same time, there was a real sense of foreboding about traveling to the remote and primitive location where the Sawi live. Two fears loomed large in traveling there: malaria mosquitoes and small airplanes.

Heading South

Although Yanti had spent her entire life in Papua, she had only the vaguest idea of where the Sawi live. So, she Googled "Sawi." Unfortunately, the Wikipedia entry for Sawi says only that the Sawi live in Papua, Indonesia. Yanti already knew that. She needed more specific information.

Her next research effort was to locate a language map of Papua and search for the Sawi language. She found it nestled in the southern coastal swamp. The nearest city with commercial air service was Merauke, in the extreme southeastern corner of Papua. So, in September 2018, she packed her backpack and bought an airline ticket to Merauke.

One Appointment Missed, Another Made

As Yanti was researching how to find the Sawi, halfway around the world in Orlando, Florida, Brent and I had an easy answer. But we were unaware of Yanti's difficulties finding the Sawi. For us, the answer was simple—go to the Mission Aviation Fellowship hangar in Sentani (Yanti's home town) and ask for a flight to Kamur village. In fact, one of my former flight students, Mike Brown, is the manager of MAF's Papua flight program! We could have simplified and shortened Yanti's journey. But if we had, we later learned that another important part of God's preparation might have been missed.

When Yanti landed in Merauke, she made her way to the boat docks to inquire about hiring a boat to get to Kamur. Unfortunately, no one in Merauke knew how to get to Kamur. They generally knew that it was "somewhere interior" from the coastline. The best they could offer was a boat trip to Agats—the next government center to the northwest up the coast.

The boat trip to Agats, not on protected interior rivers but on the open ocean, required two days of hard travel. The winds were strong, and the seas were rough. As the boat made its way into the port in Agats, Yanti snapped a photo of the scene with her camera phone. Her first inquiries about getting from Agats to Kamur were met with discouraging stares. No one seemed to know how to get to Kamur. That evening Yanti posted her arrival photo to Facebook. Soon thereafter, as she scrolled through Facebook, Yanti noticed a comment from someone named Enok asking if she was in Agats. Enok is from Sentani, as is Yanti, but he is the Chief of Police in Agats! He told Yanti she was to report to the police station the next morning. With fear and trembling, Yanti phoned Christov to ask him for prayer and counsel. She had no idea what to expect at the meeting with the police chief in the morning.

Unexpected Allies Gather

Yanti arrived to a cordial welcome by Enok. She was not in trouble, certainly not under arrest. Enok was just curious why someone from Sentani was so far from home in Agats. As Yanti explained the purpose of her travels, and her search for the Sawi, Enok called some of his staff officers into the conversation. One of the officers, Irwan, was stationed in Kamur. Within a few minutes a plan came together for Yanti to have a police escort by Irwan on the short airplane flight from Agats to Kamur!

From there, things started happening quickly. Irwan knew of Don Richardson's history and reputation among the Sawi. So, he phoned his police colleagues in Kamur to fill them in on the plan. A local police officer in Kamur, Yulianus, got the message and immediately began contacting Sawi church leaders. "Don Richardson's 'daughter' is coming to visit!"

The next call Irwan made was to Rini, the wife of another Kamur police officer, Thomas. Irwan knew that Rini was in Agats visiting her daughter at boarding school and that she was also flying back to Kamur on the next flight. The three of them met together for the return flight.

A Providential Airport Meeting

It turned out that just before the airplane landed in Agats, it had stopped in Kamur to pick up passengers. Among them was Pastor Domingus, the head of the Sawi classis of 15 Christian churches.

Domingus was just a small child when the Richardsons left Kamur. His grandfather, Sieri, was the one who warned Don about the potential for failure in the peace child exchange if they were not protected. His father, Badan, was one of the first Christian believers and pastors in Seremeet. Domingus remembered that as a young child, he was personally commissioned by Don from Isaiah 55:11. "So is my word that goes out from my mouth; It will not return to me empty but will accomplish what I desire and achieve the purpose for which I sent it." God's Word has always been dear to Domingus.

When Domingus got off the plane and made his way into the arrival area, there was already a buzz about Don Richardson's "daughter" (spiritually, not physically) waiting for the return flight to Kamur. Yanti greeted Domingus and explained her purpose in traveling to Kamur. "We want to know if you would like to translate the Old Testament."

Domingus said, "My heart shook when I heard her question. OF COURSE we want the Old Testament! We've been wanting it for 50 years!"

As Yanti, Rini, and Irwan walked toward the airplane, Domingus got on his cell phone and called several Sawi pastors and told them about the opportunity to translate the Old Testament. By the time Yanti's flight landed on the airstrip in Kamur, a welcoming party of more than 100 people was waiting for her.

They were shocked when they realized Don's "daughter" was Papuan!

Shocking News

"How is Don? Tell us about Don."

The Sawi had not heard of Don's illness. The last time they had seen Don was six years prior, during their 50th anniversary celebration in 2012. When Yanti told them about Don's cancer diagnosis they were shocked. Although their understanding of cancer is limited, their understanding of death is not. The impact of the news quickly sank in.

Yanti said, "Don wants his 'sons' and 'daughters' to continue Bible translation and to translate the Old Testament into Sawi. I am just Don's mouth to say this for him."

She was swallowed by the crowd. They embraced her as Don's "daughter" and embraced her as their Papuan sister. They embraced one another for strength in facing the news of Don's illness. They embraced the joyful prospect of having the Old Testament in Sawi. They realized that God was answering their prayers for His Word for the past 50 years. Mixed emotions overwhelmed them.

Aftershocks

"You will do the translation," Yanti said. The Sawi stared at her, speechless, unsure that they understood what she was saying.

"I know you have doubts, but God will enable you. We will bring a team to teach you how to do this." As they listened, they slowly began to realize that they had indeed heard her correctly. She was telling them that they could translate the Old Testament themselves.

So many questions. Who would do the translation? How would they spread the word and recruit translators? Where would they work? How many people would be needed? How long would it take? What would they eat? Where would they sleep? How much would it cost?

The Sawi leaders told Yanti, "Our New Testament was translated combining two Sawi dialects. We have five dialects, and we need the Bible in all of them. Our New Testament is now so old it also needs revision. We don't speak that way any more. Can we translate the whole Bible in all five of our dialects?"

What had from the outside appeared to be a potential need for Old Testament translation was quickly unfolding to be a larger need for whole Bible translations in multiple dialects. We have seen this elsewhere many times before. Local perspectives on what is needed and valued are often different than the judgments and expectations of outsiders.

Yanti responded, "We will teach you how to do Bible translation, and you can do all of these translations in the coming years. When do you want to begin?"

Their response: "Immediately!"

"How many bilingual translators can you recruit?"

"We can easily get 500!"

Yanti replied, "That might be more than we can handle. Can you recruit 150 translators?"

"Easily!" they responded.

"Ok. I think we can handle training 150 people. It will take a little time to plan all the details. Can you start next month?" Yanti asked.

"Of course! We'll be here!" the Sawi leaders concluded.

So, during the first conversation, on the first day Yanti arrived in Kamur, the Sawi church was ready to start translating Scripture. Their thirst for God's Word had been awakened by the New Testament, but they yearned for the full testimony of God. They had always assumed that only a foreigner could translate Scripture. But as they considered the opportunity ahead, they also recognized God's preparation in their lives over the past 50 years. They were no longer cannibals. They were no longer infants in the faith. They were disciples of Jesus Christ, mature students of God's Word, and witnesses to the world of God's redeeming power. They had waited 50 years for this day. They are the Sawi Christian church—God's ambassadors and servants.

The date was set. Yanti would return with the MAST training team by mid-October. The translation workshop would be from October 20-31, 2018.

10

Preparing for the Workshop

Local Logistics

Yanti had about a month to prepare for what was anticipated to be the largest single-language Bible translation
workshop in world history. The extremely remote location of
Kamur further increased the complexity. Training, equipping, feeding, and housing 150 Sawi translators would
be a tremendous undertaking. Fortunately, Yanti's years
of managing road construction teams in remote areas of
Papua gave her the logistical experience she needed to pull
this together.

Before leaving Kamur, Yanti asked the Sawi church leaders to begin making the necessary arrangements for the travel and accommodations for all the Sawi translators. Kamur has no hotels or guesthouses. It has family houses. The largest buildings in Kamur are the church, the school, the hospital, and the police station. The church was the natural place to host the workshop. The community school buildings, located next door to the church, offered two valuable support functions for the workshop. First, the school furniture could be carried from the school to the church so that the translators would have desks and chairs. Second, the empty classrooms could be used as dormitories for some of the visiting Sawi translators.

Kamur has no restaurants. It has a few small stores for packaged goods, but the Sawi get most of their food fresh from the surrounding rainforest. How would they feed all the translators and trainers? Rini, the policeman's wife who had accompanied Yanti on the flight from Agats to Kamur, volunteered to recruit a team of Sawi women to cook the meals in her home kitchen. The task was daunting. At least two hundred people eating three meals would require preparing six hundred meals per day. Then, simply repeat that every day for two weeks! Rini and Yanti calculated that they would need around 4400 pounds of food during the workshop!

Fresh water was another major challenge. Although Kamur is situated on the banks of the Kronkel and Tumdu Rivers, and it rains hundreds of inches of rain during a year, each family catches rainwater for their own use. There is no community reservoir, filtration, or distribution. There is also no sewage or waste management system. That means the river water is unpotable. The timing of the MAST workshop was set during October—just before the rainy season would begin. This would make travel and logistics easier, but it would mean fresh water would be scarce. A two-pronged plan was developed. First, Yanti purchased a dozen heavy plastic drums, each with the capacity to hold 200 liters of clean water, to increase the local clean-water storage in case the rains began early. Second, they purchased 4000 liters of packaged drinking water for the workshop participants.

Electricity is still a scarce commodity in Kamur. There is no public electrical utility or distribution system. Some stores and families own generators to power various commercial and personal priorities. A few of the more entrepreneurial owners of generators allow neighbors, for a small fee, to connect to their "power grid" with whatever wiring they can improvise and maintain. The MAST workshop would take place during daylight hours, but electrical power would be needed to power a sound system, to charge tablet computers and phones, and to power printers. A small gasoline-powered generator would handle the workload.

One more item would be essential for the facilitation team—rubber boots. If it did rain, the foot-worn paths of Kamur would immediately become muddy canals. Kneehigh rubber boots would replace the fashionable leather shoes of the visiting city folk. The Sawi were used to wading barefoot through the water.

There was no way to source all this locally, so Yanti networked with suppliers in Agats and hired boats to deliver the food and supplies to Kamur by mid-October.

Preparing for the Training

The anticipated group of 150 translators would be divided into teams of three or four translators working together on their translation assignments. Each small group would need a MAST facilitator to assist with organizing the work and tracking the progress. That meant they would need 40 to 45 facilitators in all. One element of the training strategy was to prepare a sufficient number of Sawi translators to serve as facilitators for the ongoing translation work that would occur following the workshop. Fourteen Sawi churches each recruited one person to be their local MAST facilitator. That meant another 25 to 30 MAST facilitators would have to be recruited from other parts of Indonesia to support the Sawi workshop.

Fortunately, with dozens of MAST workshops held in Indonesia over the prior year, more than 100 Indonesians already had the experience needed to assist the Sawi. Sierra started by recruiting her own brother and sister. Then she put the word about the upcoming MAST workshop out on WhatsApp, a networking program for communicating with her contacts. Many of these Indonesian facilitators knew the *Peace Child* story and were excited by the opportunity to connect with the Sawi. Within a short time, Sierra had 28 MAST facilitators and 9 other support personnel confirmed to support the October MAST workshop.

Once the commitments were made, the facilitators began their own preparations for the journey. Most had never flown on a small airplane before. Because no airlines serve Kamur, the only travel options were days by boat or minutes by Mission Aviation Fellowship's small planes. Each facilitator made airline reservations to get to Merauke, and MAF scheduled a floatplane to ferry the trainers the 200 miles from Merauke to Kamur. Flying on a small plane required each of them to strictly limit their personal baggage and to provide their body weight for MAF's flight planning.

As aviation fear and excitement converged in the hearts and minds of the facilitators, dread was their only emotional response to the anticipation of voracious swarms of tropical mosquitoes. Each facilitator surveyed their networks for effective homemade mosquito repellents and raided their local stores for commercial options. They stocked up on antimalarial medicines and prayed earnestly for God's protection.

In the meantime, Christov rallied the technical support team to purchase 40 computer tablets, load them all with our Bible Translation Writer software and resources, and ship them to Merauke for MAF transport to Kamur along with the MAST facilitation team.

God Will Make a Way

One additional, important preparation Yanti made for the upcoming workshop was to contact the president of the Papuan church denomination with whom the Sawi churches are affiliated. The connection was important both as a matter of protocol and to introduce him to the opportunity for other Papuan churches to translate Scripture in their languages. Through his many years of experience in church leadership, Pastor Dorman was well aware of the history and impact of Bible translation in Papua and for the Sawi people. However, he did not know about the growing movement of churches within Indonesia that had begun using MAST to translate Scripture into hundreds of languages. As Yanti explained MAST to him and described the resulting progress in Bible translation, Pastor Dorman enthusiastically gave his support for the Sawi churches to undertake this work.

Just one day before the MAST facilitators gathered in Papua, Pastor Dorman asked Yanti for another meeting. During the weeks since they had first met to discuss the Sawi Bible translation workshop, Pastor Dorman had been contacted by individuals who leveled harsh criticisms against the MAST movement. None of these individuals had any personal experience with MAST, but they were familiar with traditional Bible translation models—similar to the method Don Richardson had originally used to translate the Sawi New Testament. They asserted that the Sawi had no authority to do translation because their New Testament was copyrighted by the Indonesian Bible Society. They accused Wycliffe Associates of various misdeeds, but primarily of incompetence. For these reasons, they asked Pastor Dorman to withdraw his support for the workshop.

When Yanti learned that Pastor Dorman had received this criticism, and wanted to meet again, she reached out to the rest of our team for counsel and prayer support. Christov said, "A storm is coming, but we have peace in our hearts." Sierra said, "God will make a way." When the prayer request reached me, I immediately went to Don for his counsel and prayer.

Don sat in his favorite recliner as I explained the developing situation. Despite continuing to eat well, he had lost a lot of weight and muscle tone due to limited physical activity. But his heart and mind were still strong. As we counseled and prayed, Don offered to record a personal message to Pastor Dorman. He spoke in Indonesian. I recorded him on my iPhone. This is the English transcription of that audio recording:

> My name is Don Richardson, who used to work as a pastor among the Sawi people in Irian Jaya. I, with the help of pastor John Mills, translated the New Testament into the Sawi language. I have heard of the intention of the Sawi people to translate the Old Testament, to add to the New Testament that both of us pastors previously translated. I want to tell you, Pastor Dorman, that I agree with this intention. I agree that Sawi people, who are also quite fluent in the Indonesian language, should do this work so that they can be blessed by having the complete Bible. I have also heard that John Mills, who now lives in Canada, is also aware of this intention and has given his approval as well. So, I hope the Old Testament may be translated into Sawi without any hindrance. Thank you, Pastor Dorman, for accepting this voice-message from me through Wycliffe Associates— whom I respect. I will look forward to the news about the progress of this important matter of Bible translation. Thank you, honored gentleman, and may the Holy Spirit add His blessings to this great cause. Until we meet again in God's kingdom.

We emailed the audio file to Yanti just prior to her meeting with Pastor Dorman, and we prayed.

The second meeting with Pastor Dorman was positive. He was grateful for the audio message and expressed his deep respect and admiration for Don. He thanked Don for his lifetime of service and support for the Sawi churches and for their participation within the Papuan denomination. Because of his position and responsibility related to hundreds of other churches across Papua, Pastor Dorman's official endorsement of MAST was creating tensions. He felt that his official endorsement was premature, but he invited Yanti to attend their denominational meetings in November to report to all the church leaders the results from the Sawi MAST workshop. Naturally that was completely agreeable to us.

Stepping Into History

Indonesian MAST facilitators from Java, Sulawesi, Kalimantan, and Papua converged in Jayapura on the Wednesday before the workshop. Christov showed the team the original *Peace Child* video filmed in 1972, just ten years after Don and Carol Richardson had arrived in Kamur—but before most of the facilitators were even born. Then Christov showed the team the video that Don and his sons had made during their last visit to Kamur in 2012, celebrating the 50th anniversary of the Richardsons' arrival there. Many of the facilitators had read *Peace Child*, all had heard the story, but until that day only Yanti had seen the Sawi people. What had been only blurry images in their minds were now getting closer and more defined. What had been a distant piece of their national history was about to become personal experience. A story that had started with God moving a young family from Canada to Kamur was opening a new chapter with Indonesians training and serving Indonesians. With great anticipation, the MAST facilitation team made the flight from Jayapura to Merauke.

On Thursday, four MAF flights ferried the facilitation team from Merauke to Kamur. As the floatplane touched down on the turbid waters of the Kronkel River, a crowd of Sawi lined the riverbanks to welcome their Indonesian brothers and sisters in Christ. Barefoot Sawi children clambered along the shore. Sawi greeters offered their visitors woven-string "noken" bags as a gift. Although the facilitators did not speak Sawi, they quickly found that Indonesian was understood by many—and that a smile and embrace would fill in any communication gaps. It was an emotional experience to arrive in Kamur, begin learning names and faces, sense the miracle of what God had already done in transforming the Sawi, and feel the anticipation of what lay ahead in the coming days.

The women facilitators were invited to stay at the family home of Irwan—the policeman that had escorted Yanti from Agats to Kamur the first time. He invited some of the men to stay at the police station while others stayed in family homes.

More Providential Appointments

In addition to making Himself known through the translation of Scripture, God often has more in store for the people in the community. We seldom know the full extent of His plan in advance.

Irwan had grown up as a Muslim in Java, but his police assignment took him and his family to Kamur. This was his first close and prolonged contact with Christians. He had heard the history of Sawi cannibalism, Don Richardson's arrival, and the peace child exchange. Daily he saw the evidence of the Sawi lives transformed by the Christian gospel. He also knew the criminals and troublemakers that persisted despite the gospel and the law. Thirteen of them were locked in jail cells at the police station.

Irwan understood that the Indonesian Christians visiting were there to teach the Sawi how to translate the Bible, and he reasoned that this created a unique opportunity for him to impact the criminals of the community. The thirteen were literally a captive audience. Irwan asked James, Steven, and David, three of the MAST facilitators, to speak with the prisoners about their lives and crimes. With nothing else to occupy the offenders, they were glad for fresh conversations with concerned strangers. During the days that followed, six of the prisoners repented and accepted Christ as their Lord and Savior!

An Important Question

Friday morning dawned hot, and getting hotter. The air was paralyzed, unwilling or unable to move under the weight of the humidity, foreshadowing the weather ahead.

Sierra and her MAST co-leader, Maria, took a walk together through Kamur village. They wanted to take in the sights, sounds, smells, and feeling of the new place and people. They prayed and talked together with great anticipation for the coming days. As they walked, they met Pastor Karel, pastor of the Kalvari Church in Kamur, along the path. Pastor Karel had been involved in the first discussions with Yanti about organizing the Bible translation workshop and was an enthusiastic advocate for the workshop among the Sawi. One of the questions Pastor Karel raised previously resurfaced. "How many translations should we do? We have five dialects." The New Testament that Don Richardson translated was actually a combination of the two dialects of Kamur and Haenam. But the other three dialects wanted their own Scripture translation as well. Should they choose one dialect? Should the translation workshop focus on the New Testament for the other dialects, or the Old Testament? Sierra and the MAST facilitation team had come prepared to lead the Old Testament translation, but ultimately they were there simply to serve the Sawi church. The Sawi church leaders would need to answer these questions before the workshop would begin.

Final Logistics

As the MAST facilitation team gathered at the church Friday morning, their thoughts turned toward preparing the work space for the translators. Kalvari (Calvary) Church is wood frame on wooden pilings, roughly 50 feet square, that was built in the 1980s. As the largest gathering place for the Sawi, it has seen a lot of heavy use over 30 years. The front left corner of the building has sunken six inches further into the soft flood-plain than the other three corners, resulting in a noticeable slant to the floor in that corner. Every inch of space would be needed for the anticipated crowd of Sawi translators.

The church chairs would be adequate for seating, but tables would be helpful to organize the work space. The school next door had dozens of suitable tables—all made locally from "ironwood." As one facilitator described them, "They are the heaviest tables on earth." So, the Friday workout for the men was moving dozens of heavy tables about 100 yards from the schoolrooms to the church—using only muscle power.

All the food and supplies that had arrived in Kamur by boat needed to be moved from the dock to various positions around the community. The rubber boots were distributed to the MAST facilitators. Water barrels and packaged drinking water were positioned near the church and dormitories. The food was channeled through every available refrigerator and freezer to Rini's home kitchen, about a half mile from the church, for daily preparation. A motorcycle was recruited for meal delivery from her home to the church. Meal preparation for the visitors began on Friday.

Two Americans

As preparations were under way for this historic MAST workshop, I dearly wanted to attend; but the best timing for the Sawi was the worst timing for me. I had several commitments on my calendar that required me to be physically present in the U.S. In theory I could have tried to squeeze a trip to Kamur in between other commitments, but 30 years of international travel experience (and my staff) warned me that it would be unwise. So, I encouraged our Vice-President of Operations, Brent Ropp, and his wife, Linda, to make the trip to represent Wycliffe Associates.

The travel route from Orlando to Merauke, Indonesia is long. The only way to get there is through Jakarta, which requires traveling about 2300 miles past Merauke and then returning. It adds about nine hours of flying time to an already long series of flights halfway around the globe. In this case, Brent and Linda met up with an Indonesian video crew we had hired from Jakarta to record the events surrounding the Sawi workshop. They traveled together from Jakarta to Merauke.

They all reached Merauke early Friday morning via commercial airlines. To travel on to Kamur, Brent and Linda needed explicit approval from the Indonesian police. This was not an issue for the Indonesians traveling in their own country, but for Americans it was required due to government concerns about potential foreign influence in sensitive Indonesian political matters. Our Indonesian team members covered this thoroughly with the police, and Brent and Linda had no problem getting the police clearance to continue to Kamur.

The MAF floatplane flew the Ropps and the video crew to Kamur late Friday morning. They arrived to another riverbank greeting ceremony. Brent was crowned with a headdress of emu feathers and welcomed by the Sawi throng. The video crew unpacked their cameras and began shooting stills and videos to capture the moment. It wasn't long before some of these arrival photos hit Facebook—even from the remote isolation of Kamur.

Back to the Questions

After Friday lunch, Brent met with the Indonesian MAST team to catch up on their planning and preparations. During that conversation, Pastor Karel's question about the dialects and translation priorities came up. Within the facilitation team there were multiple perspectives on how best to proceed. Each option had pros and cons. But at the end of the conversation, Brent rightly observed, "It's really a question that the Sawi leaders need to answer. We are here to serve them." So, word was sent out requesting a meeting to be held on Saturday between the MAST facilitation team and the Sawi church leaders.

Opening Ceremony

Saturday morning dawned clear and hot. This would be a constant theme throughout the workshop. Anticipation for the day, and days, ahead was at its peak.

Not long after sunrise, the Sawi translators began arriving from other villages. Canoes multiplied on the riverbank as they gathered. The Sawi in Kamur led the welcome and greetings for their brothers and sisters. Spontaneous, enthusiastic reunions among friends and families broke out with wide smiles, muscular embraces, and loud voices. Strangers were introduced and similarly embraced. The growing crowd converged in front of Kalvari Church. By 9 a.m. there were 130 Sawi translators, each personally selected to represent his or her respective village and church, 37 Indonesian MAST facilitators and support personnel, and Brent and Linda—the only Americans.

With a quorum present, everyone was eager to begin. The throng of 169 migrated into the church. Within a few minutes the temperature and humidity inside matched everyone's breath.

Undaunted by the heat, the congregation united in worship. Acoustic guitars strummed in rhythm, voices soared, and hearts followed. The Indonesian and Sawi languages were interwoven in a seamless verbal tapestry. Pastor Paulus led the opening worship and offered the official welcome to all the visitors. Three Sawi elders each followed with their own greetings and exhortations. Then they invited Brent to the platform to hear from him. After offering words of encouragement from Scripture, translated into Sawi for the audience, Brent announced that someone else wanted to speak to them about the Bible translation they were about to begin.

A Word From Don

After correcting a mix-up on the appropriate generator fuel, electrical power was available to run the video projector. Don and his son Steve had each pre-recorded short video messages for the Sawi and sent them along with Brent.

The entire room was silent out of deep respect and anticipation for Don's words. When his face was projected onto the wall and his voice began speaking to them, many of the Sawi instinctively reached their hands toward the screen as if to touch him. Across the entire crowd, the love and respect of the Sawi for Don was overflowing from their hearts onto their faces. They held their breath to hear every word Don said.

Don's message to them was simple. He encouraged them to do the work of Bible translation with faith, humility, and diligence. He reminded them of God's transforming work in their lives and of their place as His children. He encouraged them to welcome the MAST facilitation team just as they had welcomed him so many years before.

When Don described his illness to them, and the fragility of his life, many of the Sawi broke down sobbing. They realized that they would likely never see Don again in this life, which was heartbreaking for them. Don said, "I'll see you in heaven. This is not 'goodbye'—it is just 'so long' until then." It was a painful, sobering way for the Sawi to begin their translation work. While their faith was strengthened by Don's words of encouragement, their hearts were grieving the time and distance that separated them from Don. They longed for more counsel and teaching from him. They yearned for another embrace. They wanted more time together, but they knew it would not happen. Don was their earthly Christian 'father', a personal friend to many of them, and they grieved his illness. They knew death was coming for Don, and they knew they were helpless to oppose it.

As Steve Richardson, their earthly Christian brother, spoke his video greetings and encouragement, it reminded the Sawi that the life of the elders is carried on in the lives of their children. Steve would soon grieve Don's passing, just as the Sawi were grieving in anticipation. But Steve, and the Sawi, would continue. They would live their lives in a way that reflected the faith and character of their father. It was part of God's plan to make Himself known to others through their lives. By the time Steve's video message concluded, the Sawi were ready. They were reassured that the task ahead, translating Scripture into Sawi, was the continuation of what God had started through Don. God had called Don to bring the Sawi the gospel and the New Testament. Over 50 years God had prepared the Sawi to steward His Word for their people. The time was right.

Introducing MAST

After lunch the MAST facilitation team began introducing the Sawi translators to more of the details of the MAST process. They described the eight steps of MAST.

There are four steps in the drafting process: 1) reading or listening to the text in the majority language (in this case Indonesian), 2) verbalizing the text in Sawi, 3) breaking the target passage into smaller, but coherent, chunks, and 4) blind drafting—putting their Sawi translation into an initial draft based on what they learned in the three prior steps.

Immediately after the drafting steps, four quality checking steps follow: 5) self-check comparing the Sawi blind draft to the Indonesian source text, 6) peer checking each others' work again comparing the Sawi blind draft to the Indonesian source text, 7) key word checking to be sure that all translators are using precisely the same word for every key theological term (sin, grace, forgiveness, etc.), and 8) verse-by-verse checking with the community and church leaders to assure that the translation is faithful to the original Biblical text.

Formal Agreements

After the steps of MAST were introduced, our team distributed copies of two documents for every translator to review and sign. The first document was our Statement of Faith, succinctly describing our commitment to biblical Christian doctrines. The second document was our Translation Guidelines, describing the broadly accepted principles upon which Bible translation is based. Within this second document is our encouragement that the translation be owned by the local church but released openly for the benefit of anyone who speaks Sawi or related languages. This is part of a broad strategy to make Scripture readily available globally with unrestricted access for all. Within this discussion it slowly became clear that some Sawi could not read the documents in Indonesian. But based on discussion, all the

Sawi signed the agreements to make their translation work available to all.

Who Has God Brought?

The rest of Saturday afternoon was spent surveying the knowledge and skills of the Sawi translators. "Authentic assessment" is an educational approach that aims to determine a student's practical knowledge and skills for a specific task. The translators were recruited and selected by the Sawi church leaders based on the leaders' assessment of their Christian faith, public testimony and trustworthiness, bilingual skills, and technical skills. But each translator brought a unique set of these skills. Our MAST team then assessed each of them to quantify further their knowledge of the Sawi language, their knowledge of the Indonesian language, their biblical understanding, and their literacy level.

One obvious outcome of the initial assessment was the recognition that each translator had unique skills to contribute to the team. It was not a matter of testing and then excluding individuals that fail a standardized test. It was a matter of creating small translation teams that included the complementary skills needed to have a quality outcome. It was a practical reflection of 1 Corinthians 12—one body with many unique, valuable, and essential parts. The good news was that God had woven together a strong team of Sawi translators: elders and youth, men and women, articulate Sawi poets and people educated formally in Indonesian, people with computer experience, graduates of Bible schools and seminaries, university graduates, and people with prayer power. Every Sawi pastor and most Sawi elders participated. They were taking the task of Bible translation very seriously, and the Sawi church was fully engaged.

Within the assessment discussion the question surfaced of how best to include Sawi women within the teams. Culturally, the Sawi women would typically be deferential to Sawi men if they were working in the same group. This approach often loses the benefit of having active input from the women. So, the decision was made to segregate the groups with men and women working on separate teams.

In preparation for the church service on Sunday morning, at dusk the men had to move all "the heaviest tables on earth" out of the church. The distance back to the school seemed too far to go, so they put them under a tent next to the church. The combination of a long day, doing assessments on 144 Sawi translators and facilitators, the tropical heat, and moving tables, left the team physically drained. But by the end of the day on Saturday, the already high sense of anticipation for what God would do through this effort had risen to even greater heights.

Answering the Questions

Since Brent had suggested that the church leaders needed to answer the questions related to translation priorities and dialect differences, a group of 20 Sawi church leaders met with him late in the afternoon. He invited Pastor Karel to restate his questions for the group and then asked them to respond. After brief discussion among the Sawi leaders, the consensus was clear. Their most urgent priority was to learn how to translate Scripture themselves and to translate the Old Testament. Once they knew how to translate themselves, they could do as many additional dialects as they would choose. "We can do the rest later. We want to do the Old Testament using the dialects Don used so that it is consistent with our New Testament." With that, the translation plan was set.

Sabbath Rest

After the busyness of Saturday, everyone wanted to rest and refresh spiritually on Sunday through worship, fellowship, and Bible study. The Sawi and the MAST facilitators spontaneously headed to the various nearby churches. Some required a bit of canoe paddling to reach. Visitors are always welcomed and invited to speak to Sawi congregations. In most cases these were brief greetings and encouragements. In at least one case it turned into an invitation to preach.

Pastor David, one of the Indonesian MAST facilitators, was invited to preach. Knowing that most of the congregation were likely Christians, but sensing God's prompting to make a clear presentation of the gospel, Pastor David did just that. He preached about the sinfulness of mankind in general and individual accountability for sin. He described the penalty for sin, alienation from God in this life and for eternity. Then he described Christ's sacrificial death for each sinner, paying the penalty to reconcile men and women to God. At the close he extended an invitation to anyone to come forward and publicly declare their faith in Jesus Christ as their Lord and Savior. Three people immediately came forward! Then, suddenly, the entire congregation rose to their feet and surrounded the new Christians with praise and worship to God for His redeeming power! Songs were sung. Prayers were lifted. Several asked to be baptized! It was a powerful reflection of God at work within the Sawi church and an encouragement to everyone who heard the testimony in the days that followed.

Sunday Afternoon

After the church gatherings dismissed, Rini's kitchen assured that no one went hungry. Her kitchen was open and working 16 hours every day for the next two weeks.

After lunch the MAST team finished their planned assignments of Sawi translators to smaller translation teams; then they began planning assignments of Old Testament books and chapters for each group to work on, beginning on Monday. Finally, they again had to move all the ironwood tables back into Kalvari Church and plan table assignments for each small translation group.

Brent and Linda took advantage of the unscheduled afternoon to see more of the Richardsons' world. Rini's husband, Thomas, volunteered to chauffer them in his speedboat. It was not as symbolic of the Richardsons' world as a dugout canoe would have been—but it was drier and much more stable! From Thomas and Rini's house on the northward stretch of the Kronkel River, the Richardsons' homesite on the Tumdu tributary was just over a mile away. Thomas slowly grounded his boat on the shore in front of their former homesite.

Brent and Linda scrambled over the front of the boat onto the shoreline and walked amid the ironwood pilings—the only remaining evidence of the Richardsons' house. Brent and Linda tried to imagine setting up housekeeping there in 1962, among cannibals. It was beyond their imagination. Around and within the pilings some enterprising Sawi had planted a small garden. Since the Richardsons were no longer using it, there seemed no reason to let this rare piece of high ground (a few feet above the high-water line) go to waste.

Thirty steps further along the Tumdu brought Brent and Linda to the hull of the Richardsons' houseboat. After building their first house, and after the peace child breakthrough illustrating God's sacrificial love for the Sawi, Don had needed a means of traveling to other Sawi villages with his apprentice evangelists to share the good news of the gospel. So, he built a houseboat. Three parallel oversized canoes formed the keels. The house, mostly just enclosed sleeping areas and a few benches for seating, was framed onto the canoe foundation. No doubt in the 1960s this houseboat left quite a wake on the local rivers. By the time Brent and Linda saw it, someone had conscripted the middle canoe for active duty. The house structure leaned heavily in the direction where tropical weather and insects had consumed the supports. Nevertheless, it was a vivid reminder of Don's dauntless pioneering and entrepreneurial spirit.

Behind the houseboat was a large unnatural clearing. In the early 1970s this had been the building site for the Sawidome, a large covered structure for which Don had created plans and supervised construction. Once peace had broken out, former enemies from distant Sawi villages wanted to move closer to receive Don's teaching. This swelled the Christian population surrounding the Richardsons and birthed a vision for a larger meeting space. At its completion the Sawidome was 75 feet in diameter under an arched roof 40 feet high. Hundreds of Sawi gathered in its shade for more than 20 years, until weather and insects brought it to ruins. Today no vestiges of the Sawidome remain. All structural poles have been repurposed for other buildings.

As the sun sank toward the horizon, the air was filled with a sense of expectation for what God would do in the days ahead.

11

Sawi MAST Workshop

The Crowd Swells

Kamur village was overflowing with visitors, and more kept coming. The 130 Sawi translators who had arrived on Saturday were joined by 81 more translators on Monday morning! Some of these had church or family commitments on Sunday so were unable to come earlier. Others had just heard about the workshop that weekend and decided to join the team. The result was that the Sawi overshot their goal of 150 translators by 40 percent! To our knowledge, this was the largest single-language Bible translation event in world history—with 211 Sawi translators!

The late arrivals added to the complexity of Monday morning. The newcomers joined the small groups already working inside the church. The priority for the morning was getting the groups organized and focusing on the four drafting steps of the MAST process for their assigned passage—consume, verbalize, chunk, and blind draft. Forty-two small groups began translating their assignments in parallel.

Things Heat Up

By mid-morning every inch of Kalvari Church was crowded with people. As the sun climbed overhead, the tropical heat was feverish. Yanti found a couple electric fans and plugged them into the makeshift wiring from the generator. The fans gave minimal relief to the groups directly in their wake, but most of the workshop participants felt no reprieve. Soon any available piece of paper or cardboard was put into service as a handheld fan. The Sawi were used to the heat, but the crowding was unpleasant even for them. For the outsiders it was very uncomfortable and distracting.

Rini's kitchen was working at full speed to prepare meals for 250 people. With no simple way to prepare sago from local resources for this number of people, Rini had ordered sacks of rice from Agats to meet the demand. Small bits of chicken and hot peppers added protein and spice. Cardboard boxes with lunches wrapped inside were stacked and tied with string to the seat of the delivery motorcycle, barely leaving enough room for the driver.

Struggling

By lunch time, cell phone calls were made to merchants in Agats to order ten more box fans for delivery by boat as soon as possible. The MAST facilitators working with each small group counseled with one another about the impact of the heat and crowded space on translation progress. Obviously, this was a very early measure; but based on experience, they were beginning to be concerned that some organizational adjustments might be needed.

One challenge that became clearer as the small groups were working was that the older Sawi were not as literate in the Indonesian source text as the younger ones were. While the younger translators could read and grasp the Indonesian text, the elders needed more discussion in Sawi to explain the verses and passages before proceeding. Only the college-age students were comfortable using the tablet computers. Some of the small groups included Sawi pastors and elders, while others did not. The groups without Sawi pastors seemed to be hesitant in their drafting, anxious for their church leaders to give them feedback before progressing. Also, the mixture of five Sawi dialects dispersed among the groups complicated their communications.

By the end of Monday, the optimism and anticipation that had started the day had melted away. The MAST steps were completely foreign to the Sawi. They wanted to please the facilitators, but they were very uncertain about how to best do that. They wanted to know that the verses they translated were done right; but because they spent most of the day just learning how to draft, they were not at all confident in their work. They worried that they might not be up to the task. The heat and crowding amplified their concerns. Most of them were away from home, working with people they did not know well, and eating what to them was foreign food. The problems and challenges were now painfully obvious. The solutions were not.

The MAST facilitation team was similarly discouraged. The physical challenges of conducting a workshop in such a remote location were overwhelming them. The best preparations they had made were inadequate to overcome all the challenges.

As the sun sank into the horizon, the facilitation team prayed. First, they prayed for rain. The rain barrels were empty. Shade was scant relief from the tropical sun. Everyone was completely dependent upon the packaged drinking water, which was exactly the same temperature and humidity as the air they were breathing. They prayed for physical relief to face the ongoing challenges. Second, they prayed for wisdom and patience as they continued to teach the Sawi the eight steps of MAST. Monday was focused on learning the drafting steps. Tuesday would be focused on learning the checking steps.

Sierra said it was the most difficult first day of any MAST workshop she had ever led. She didn't know then that it was going to get worse before it got better.

From Bad to Worse

Overnight about 60 of the Sawi translators became ill. Many were experiencing headaches and stomach aches. Some had more pernicious vomiting and diarrhea. The hospital and clinic filled up overnight.

Brent sent me an email asking us to mobilize a prayer response. Within a few hours people worldwide were fighting the spiritual battle in prayer.

As Tuesday began, all the Sawi translation groups were missing participants. The physical and emotional stress was high. It wasn't long before someone noticed that none of the MAST facilitators were sick. Only Sawi were sick. Someone else commented that they noticed the facilitators were not eating the same food as the Sawi on Monday. The Sawi meals were wrapped in banana leaves, but a few meals for the visitors were wrapped in paper.

"The foreigners are poisoning us! They have fattened us for the slaughter!" It was a suspicion that resurfaced from deep in their own dark history. Many times they had deceived their enemies, pretending to be friends, only to kill them unexpectedly. Before Christ, deception and treachery had been the pinnacle of Sawi ideals.

"No. This is Satan trying to divide and discourage us. These are our Indonesian brothers and sisters. They are eating the same food we are, but in paper instead of banana leaves." The Sawi church leaders calmed their congregations.

New theories of the mysterious sickness began surfacing. Sago is the starchy staple of most Sawi diets. Rice is definitely foreign to them. Rini is originally from Sulawesi, not Papua. She probably used more peppers than the Sawi expected to spice up her cooking. Rini got the word to lighten up on the spices, and she adjusted her recipes accordingly.

To reassure everyone, the MAST facilitators ate together with their Sawi translation groups. Someone found a box of plastic spoons and distributed them to the Sawi to reduce potential food contamination from their hands. Boxes of tissues circulated to clean their hands before and after the meals.

The depleted translation workforce pressed on and gained some experience with the MAST checking steps. But during the day another 30 Sawi translators took ill and headed to the clinic. It felt like the workshop itself was infected. What had started as the most difficult first day had extended to become the most difficult opening two days of any MAST workshop.

Regrouping

By God's grace, many of the Sawi who had been stricken ill were recovering by Wednesday morning. Instead of losing more translators overnight, the translation groups were returning to their former size and strength. Rumors of poisoning evaporated. The fans arrived by boat from Agats. As the translation groups worked through all eight steps of the MAST process, their confidence in the quality increased.

After a few days working in groups that included speakers from multiple Sawi dialects, the Sawi MAST facilitators-in-training brought a suggestion to the rest of the facilitation team. Since each of the 14 facilitators-in-training represented a Sawi church in a different village, they suggested that the translation groups be reconfigured based on these villages. That would allow people of the same dialect to understand one another more easily and would set the stage for the post-workshop translation to continue at each of the village churches. The facilitation team immediately began working to realign the teams based on their input.

They decided to reduce the number of translation groups from 42 to 23. This meant that every group would include more than one Sawi church leader, increasing their faith and confidence to proceed. It also meant that instead of translating 42 passages in parallel, they were working on only 23 passages at a time. That would slow the progress during the workshop but likely improve the progress after the workshop.

When the plan to regroup was brought to the entire translation team, the wisdom was clear to the Sawi community. The realignment happened mid-afternoon on Wednesday, giving the small groups time to work together with people from their own villages and dialects. Once this realignment occurred, a new dynamic became clear—Sawi leaders were already leading the Sawi Bible translation. The MAST facilitation team continued to encourage, coach, and serve the Sawi translation groups. But on the third day of working together in Bible translation—MAST had become Sawi.

Ropps' Departure

On Wednesday Brent and Linda Ropp were catching an MAF flight back to Merauke and then continuing homeward to Orlando to attend other organizational priorities. The MAF floatplane was in the shop for maintenance; so Mike Brown, the MAF Papua Program Manager, landed on the Kamur airstrip early Wednesday morning. After 20 years serving mission organizations and Papuan churches, Mike was curious to see MAST in action. His fluency in Indonesian enabled him to understand quickly the mood of the Sawi participants. Seeing the crowd of Sawi, engaged in Bible translation as an entire community, was a stirring experience.

Before departing, Brent wanted to get a copy of some of the Sawi Old Testament translation to take back to Don. Because of the difficulties of the first two days, most of the translations were still early drafts needing to continue through the four checking steps. As Brent and Linda made their way around the translation groups, they came upon a group translating the book of Nehemiah.

A young woman, Natalia, was in the group. Natalia is the adult daughter of Isai, who as a young boy hid in the tree-tops when Don first arrived and later became an evangelist and translation assistant for the Sawi New Testament. The group had just drafted Nehemiah chapter 8—the story of Ezra opening the Scriptures to read for all the Israelites after many years without it. This passage seemed a fitting reflection of the moment to present later to Don.

When word of the Ropps' imminent departure spread among the translators, everyone wanted a photo opportunity. Individuals, small groups, and larger groups spontaneously gathered around Brent and Linda to capture the moment. Cell phones materialized from pockets and noken bags for the obligatory selfies. Mike, Brent, and Linda had to withdraw politely from the church to help the translation groups refocus on the task at hand. There was still a week of workshop left to complete and lots of Old Testament Scripture to draft and check.

Brent's Reflections

As the engine power peaked and Mike released the brakes, the MAF plane gathered momentum and let go of the runway—rising gently on the wind. Brent looked out the window as Kamur fell away, another profound chapter written in his life and ministry.

Forty-two years after first meeting Don Richardson during a speaking engagement at Grace College where Brent attended, Brent's ministry journey took him to the very same village, paths, and people where Don had served so many years before. Despite the intervening years, the place had remained much the same—distant, isolated, difficult, and daunting. Seeing the place, and imagining the Richardsons' first arrival, further increased Brent and Linda's already high respect for the Richardsons' faith and action.

What was impossible to imagine was the difference in the people. When Don arrived in 1962, the Sawi were expert liars and killers. Today the Sawi are people of love and peace. The gospel, and 50 years of living according to God's Word, so thoroughly transformed them that it is difficult to remember their wicked past. Since they stopped killing each other, a tribe of 2,000 cannibals has become a community of 10,000 Christians!

The unity and engagement of the Sawi church in translating Scripture was inspiring, reflecting the power of the Holy Spirit to transform people from death to life and showing that no one is beyond redemption.

As he saw Kamur disappear beyond the horizon, and the canopy of jungle below hid any evidence of the people living there, Brent wondered how long it would be before God's Word would reach the Sawi's neighbors.

Pressing On

As the workshop continued, the Sawi gained momentum and confidence in their work. Translations grew from verses to passages, to chapters, and books. Teams were simultaneously translating 22 Old Testament books: Exodus, Leviticus, Numbers, Ruth, Nehemiah, Esther, Proverbs, Ecclesiastes, Song of Solomon, Daniel, Hosea, Joel, Amos, Obadiah, Jonah, Micah, Nahum, Habakkuk, Zephaniah, Haggai, Zechariah, and Malachi. Naturally the shorter books required less time for drafting and checking; but each time a book was completed, the enthusiasm increased and the next book was undertaken.

One of the women Sawi facilitators, Ribka, excitedly messaged her husband, Andy, about the translation progress. Andy was away in Agats when the MAST workshop began but decided to return to Kamur when he heard the news. Ribka asked him to help check their group's translation work. When he saw the progress firsthand, he was so moved that he volunteered to help translate. Since Andy is a worship leader and songwriter, it seemed natural to ask him to begin working on the Psalms. As he prayed about how to begin, God impressed on him to begin with Psalm 119—the longest chapter in the Bible with 176 verses. Andy was inspired. He drafted and checked all 176 verses of Psalm 119 in just two days!

During the evenings, after the light became too dim to continue working, the Sawi asked, "Can we see the video from Don again? Could we see the *Peace Child* video again as well?" So, the evenings became a time to reminisce and reflect on the grace of God in moving Don to Kamur. The elders retold stories of Sawi history, and the younger ones wondered at how different their lives might have been if God had not reached out to them.

From New to Old

The four checking steps of MAST are essential: 1) self check, 2) peer check, 3) key word check, and 4) verse-by-verse check. The first two checking steps assure that nothing was unintentionally omitted, or inserted, during the blind draft step. These are a comparison between the newly translated minority language text and the majority language source texts being used.

The third checking step, the key word check, assures agreement and harmony among all translators in the use of key terms. As you can imagine, with 211 Sawi translators working, the potential for using different terminology to describe similar things was very high. This same challenge even existed for the original writers of Scripture. Dozens of writers working over hundreds of years in widely varying circumstances could easily have resulted in confusing or contradictory references and descriptions. But the Holy Spirit sovereignly guided and guarded their Hebrew, Greek, and Aramaic words. During MAST translation workshops, we always pray for the Holy Spirit to continue guiding and guarding the work, and the key word check is an essential part of the due diligence in following His guidance.

Having had the New Testament for 50 years, the Sawi are extremely knowledgeable of its teachings and terminology. We could rightly say that their understanding of God has been primarily shaped by their understanding of Jesus Christ. There is certainly nothing wrong with this—but it presented a bit of a challenge to some of the Sawi translators.

As they began drafting Old Testament passages and naturally came to verses about God, some of them defaulted to their most familiar Sawi name for God—*Yesus*. Jesus was their first thought when thinking of God. There is truth and beauty in this theology, but it is not sound translation. It also highlights the essential value of each checking step in MAST.

This is not the kind of translation mistake that would be easily caught in a self check. Because the individuals who translated God using the word *Yesus* in their blind draft follow with a self check, they would not immediately recognize their mistake. To them this obviously seemed like the right word. The place where this mistake was immediately recognized was in the peer check and key word checking steps. When their Sawi neighbor read their translation draft using the word *Yesus* for God, they might ask, "Why did you use *Yesus* instead of *Myao Kodon*?" During the key word discussion, the agreement of both the church leaders and the entire Sawi community was that *Myao Kodon* was the only correct Sawi term for Almighty God. After this discussion, these translation mistakes were corrected, and *Myao Kodon* flowed naturally into the continuing Scripture drafts.

Real and Perceived Threats

By midweek the MAST facilitators were getting more casual about using mosquito repellant. With no sign of rain, they also began leaving their rubber boots behind and went barefoot alongside the Sawi. Former strangers were becoming fast friends. Uncertainty and fear grew into trust and familiarity. God was knitting His people together to do His work.

One morning as the translation teams were working, a young Sawi mother was abruptly called away due to an emergency—her child had been bitten by a snake. The Sawi all knew the dire implications. The venom of one species of snake in their region is so toxic that death occurs within 30 minutes. No one has ever recovered from the bite of that snake. The mother ran to where her child was lying on the bank of the Tumdu River. The child was crying in pain but didn't seem to be losing consciousness. That was the first encouraging sign. As the mother polled all the other nearby children, the consensus seemed to be that her child was bitten while splashing in the river—not on land. That was the second encouraging sign. The common river snakes are not poisonous. The mother carried her child almost a mile to the clinic. There was no anti-venin for the poison, but the nurse was able to assess the child's condition. Breathing and vision were normal. As the minutes passed, the child's pain subsided, and it became clear that this was not a poisonous snake bite.

The next day, all the Indonesian MAST facilitators began wearing their rubber boots again.

Time Flies

Translation continued that week through Saturday, giving the participants two days of training and illness followed by four days of drafting and checking. Morale was once again high with the sense that the Holy Spirit had seen them through the challenging initial days, had helped them climb the translation learning curve, and was enabling them to translate Scripture with excellence. Everyone was excited to see the growing stack of translated Old Testament books.

Since most of the translators worked using paper and pen, typing the translations into the computer tablets became an increasing priority by the end of the week. The technical team was working late into the nights collecting the completed translations, checking the formatting, assuring that every chapter and book had the correct number of verses and chapters, and preparing them for printing before the end of the workshop.

Everyone paused for worship on Sunday morning, but by afternoon many had concluded that Bible translation was not a compromise to honoring the Lord's Day. They were back at their tables translating Scripture on Sunday afternoon, redeeming the time for maximum progress. Translation was no longer hard work. It was a labor of love for their people.

Printing would have to be done on Tuesday in order to distribute the completed work to the translators on Wednesday before the close of the workshop. That meant the printing priorities had to be settled by the end of work on Monday.

By sunset on Monday, eleven Old Testament books had been completed, four more were nearing completion, and seven other books were progressing through the drafting and checking steps. Typists were working hard to get the handwritten translations entered into the computer tablets in preparation for printing.

Tuesday morning, as the translation teams continued to work at Kalvari Church, the Print-On-Demand system was set up at the police station, tested, and immediately put to work. Though good progress was made during the day, it was not without challenges. Keeping the generator fueled and running, clearing printer misfeeds, refilling printer ink, adding paper, collating the pages for each book, and continuing to quality check the print files kept the print team busy. The sun set Tuesday evening, but the print team kept working. Three team members worked through the entire night without sleeping.

The Workshop Conclusion

Preparations had been made for an afternoon celebration to mark the completion of the workshop on Wednesday, October 31. That meant there was still time Wednesday morning for more Bible translation. The Sawi translation teams joyfully continued their work, even while anticipating the celebration to come. By the end of the morning they had completed four more books, for a total of 15 Old Testament books and Psalm 119 translated in 8-1/2 days of work. They were THRILLED!

Before the celebration, many Sawi translators changed into traditional ceremonial costumes. As they gathered outside Kalvari Church, the energy and excitement were high. Shouts of jubilation echoed through the crowd. Singing and dancing spontaneously broke out. Tears of joy overflowed. Cell phone cameras captured every moment in videos, stills, and selfies.

The printed Old Testament books naturally had a prominent place in the celebration. Eleven complete books, plus Psalm 119, had been printed. The translators from Haenam village ceremoniously handed the printed books to Yanti, who then passed them along to the translators from the other villages to symbolize the spread of God's Word through all Sawi villages. Two copies of each book were printed for each of the 15 Sawi churches. Inside Kalvari Church several translators and church leaders stood to testify about the impact of the workshop on them personally and the importance of the Old Testament translation for the Sawi people.

The overwhelming sense was that the Sawi had begun writing a new chapter in their history. Former generations of Sawi had been cannibals. This generation of Sawi had become Bible translators, opening the path for all future generations of Sawi to be stewards of God's Word for their people.

Sad Farewells

On Thursday the Indonesian MAST facilitators began their journeys homeward. A crowd of Sawi translators and church leaders bid them farewell at the airport with several more rounds of selfies and exchanges of WhatsApp or Facebook contact information.

Hanging heavy over the moment was the news of the fatal Lion Air crash in Jakarta just three days prior, killing 189 passengers and crew members. Several of the MAST facilitators were scheduled to fly Lion Air from Sentani to other destinations in Indonesia. As they admitted their fears to the MAF pilot, he reassured them that because of the accident, Lion Air was among the safest airlines in the world at that moment. Every Lion Air pilot would be carefully monitoring every system and following every safety procedure in the wake of that accident.

After facing their fears and uncertainty, and overcoming many challenges during the workshop, they all shared a deep sense of blessing and privilege in having met and worked with the Sawi. For some who had read *Peace Child* in earlier years, the realization that God had woven them into the tapestry of Sawi history was life changing. For others the theory of being an instrument in God's hand had been translated into reality. They sensed God's anointing, His enabling, and His power at work in and through them—in a new way.

12

AFTER THE WORKSHOP

Reporting to Don

When Brent and Linda returned to Orlando, I phoned Don to see when we could all meet to hear the Ropps' account of their time with the Sawi. By the end of October, Don's physical strength was noticeably declining, but his spirit and mind were still strong. He was excited to hear Brent's report from the Sawi.

Brent handed Don the Sawi draft of Nehemiah 8. It took some adjusting for Don to get his eyes focused. He immediately read through the passage and wondered aloud about some of the verb tenses and noun forms. Brent reminded him that this draft was from very early during the workshop and had not been through the MAST checking steps. It was exciting to see Don's energy and engagement as he read the translation. For a few moments it was as though he was transported back to his days in Kamur working on the Sawi New Testament.

Don, Brent, Linda, Jan, and I sat quietly together soaking in the significance of the moment.

"Don, the Sawi are continuing what God began through you. The Sawi church is now the steward of God's Word for the Sawi people," I affirmed.

Brent reflected, "Seeing where you lived, imagining your life there among cannibals, increased my already immense respect for what you did there. Experiencing the unity and enthusiasm of the Sawi church was exhilarating! Meeting old men who were just young boys when you arrived and seeing generations of Sawi who have lived their lives peacefully under the teaching of God's Word was impressive! It was so humbling to be a part of the same story God began writing through you."

There was no stage or spotlight, no crowd or applause. Don sat in his living room, in his favorite chair, wearing a comfortable plaid shirt, quietly holding a single page of Nehemiah 8 translated into Sawi.

It was a holy moment.

I felt then, and I feel now, that I didn't deserve to be there. I felt like I was trespassing in private space that belonged rightly to God and Don. That they each invited me to be there with them can only be described as undeserved grace.

Brent recounted stories of the Sawi he had met, the conversations he'd had, and the challenges the Sawi faced during the opening days of the MAST workshop. Don brightened with the mention of each name, his mind picturing those he had seen at the reunion in 2012.

Eventually our conversation naturally turned to prayer for the Sawi. They were off to a good start but had a lot of hard work still ahead before they would complete their translation of the Old Testament. Our closing "amen" seemed to have unique eternal magnitude—as though we were just beginning to see what God had already accomplished in His providence.

Papuan Church Conference

Once back in Sentani, Yanti arranged to meet Pastor Dorman to give him a full account of the Sawi Bible translation workshop. When she reported that the Sawi had completed 15 Old Testament books during 8-1/2 days of work, Pastor Dorman was speechless. Bible translation in his own language began almost 20 years ago and does not yet have this much Scripture completed.

Pastor Dorman again extended his invitation for Yanti to attend the November 2018 denominational conference of the Gospel Churches of Indonesia. Because of the continuing need for Bible translation in more than 100 Papuan languages and the interest stirred among the pastors by the Sawi translation workshop, Bible translation became an important agenda item for that conference. Pastor Dorman also invited representatives from two other Bible translation organizations to attend and participate in the discussions.

The church conference was held in the Papuan mountain village of Bokondini because of its central location. During the days immediately preceding the conference, tensions increased in the community after the unexplained deaths of four local men. This understandably concerned the church leaders who were converging in Bokondini for the conference. Pastor Dorman had arrived a few days ahead of the conference with his planning team. Rumors prowled the local streets searching for any explanation of the deaths. As the situation deteriorated, Pastor Dorman contacted Yanti to dissuade her from traveling to Bokondini. But Yanti persisted. She felt that God had opened the door for her to connect with these evangelical pastors so that their language groups could have His Word sooner. So, she took the MAF flight from Sentani to Bokondini.

The morning Yanti arrived, the security situation in Bokondini was precarious. The police and military were tense. Local citizens were brandishing weapons and taunting the authorities. To make matters worse, as people searched for someone to blame for the deaths, Pastor Dorman became a target for rumors. He was harassed and followed. When he met Yanti at the airport he said, "You are the only Bible translator who has come. All the others canceled. Thank you for coming here to be with us!" But as they surveyed the growing threats surrounding them, Pastor Dorman compelled Yanti to return to Sentani on an afternoon flight. He wanted to be sure she was safe so that she could continue to advance Bible translation throughout Papua. After Yanti's departure, Pastor Dorman was questioned by the police. But since he had nothing to do with the deaths, they found no evidence and released him.

Despite the rumors and uncertainty, many Papuan pastors stayed to meet. As expected, Bible translation figured prominently in their conversations. The Sawi pastors provided their denominational colleagues a progress report on the Sawi Old Testament translation. Dozens of Papuan pastors were encouraged and emboldened by the report from the Sawi church leaders and became intent on launching Bible translation in their respective languages as soon as possible.

Interviewing Don

One of Don's doctors encouraged him to expect to celebrate Christmas 2018 but said he likely should not plan for Christmas in 2019. With each visit to Don I could see subtle changes in his posture, breathing, and memory. I cleared my schedule to spend as much time with him as possible. I knew that Don Richardson's perspectives on life, faith, and ministry were limited commodities that I wanted to soak in.

During the fall of 2018 we met several times at his home. Don told me that the Sawi Old Testament translation and my plan to write their story gave him something to look forward to during those days. We reflected on the *Peace Child* story, God's work in and through the Sawi after his family's departure, and on his years of writing and speaking about missions and ministry. We talked about the impact MAST had in getting Scripture to hundreds of languages. We talked about our kids and grandkids. We prayed together. As we talked about this book, Don also asked Carol to make a few minor revisions to his own memoirs. These were precious times and conversations.

By November a new dynamic had come into play. As Don continued to lose strength and experienced dizziness and disorientation, falls in his home became more frequent. Carol was unable to lift him but a neighbor or the local emergency squad just down the street was glad to respond and assist with getting Don back into his chair or bed. The growing stress was taking a toll on both Don and Carol. Jan and I offered to stay with Don for an evening so that Carol could take a brief break and enjoy a Christmas concert. We shared a meal alone with Don. After dinner I helped him make his way to bed. It was heartbreaking to see this giant of a man becoming steadily weaker.

Christmas

Our extended family began converging at our home a week ahead of Christmas. One evening we rallied our kids, grandkids, and Jan's parents for Christmas caroling around the neighborhood. Our hope was to sing for Don and Carol, but when we stopped at their home there was no answer at the door. Later we learned they had indeed been home but didn't hear our knock from within Don's back bedroom.

On Saturday morning, December 22, Carol phoned me to ask for help getting Don from his chair to his bed. When I arrived, he was seated next to the bed. Carol and I stood at his sides to lift and steady him, but without his effort we could not lift him from the chair. For what seemed an agonizingly long time, Don pressed his hands against the arms of the chair with all his remaining strength, slowly rising to stand. We helped him turn and sit on the side of the bed, then lifted his legs as he shifted to lie down. He was exhausted.

Because of his fatigue I stayed just a few moments with him. He was looking forward to the arrival of one of his sons and two grandsons and spoke of his desire to encourage them in their faith. We prayed together for his grandkids. When I returned home, I confided to Jan that I felt I had seen Don exert his last ounce of strength and that I suspected he likely would not be able to get out of bed again.

That evening his anticipated family members arrived and Don enjoyed a brief conversation with them. Less than an hour later, he experienced the onset of increasing physical distress. Early the following morning—Sunday, December 23, 2018—Don passed from this life to the Next.

That morning as I was getting ready for church, I received a text message from Don's son Steve that Don had passed away. Although I had known his death was imminent, reading the text still took my breath away. I wept for the loss of a great missionary statesman and dear friend.

With the extended family gathered for the holidays, the Richardsons decided to have a private graveside service on Thursday, December 27. Jan and I were invited to attend. We were blessed to see Don's family members gathered together and to hear reflections on the life and personal impact of their father and grandfather.

Don was always an encourager to me. He graciously invited me to come close. He listened and counseled. He challenged

13

In Kamur

Getting Close

Since I had not been able to attend the October 2018 Sawi MAST workshop, I asked our team to inquire with the Sawi church leaders regarding timing for a subsequent visit. Consensus began building toward an early January 2019 visit to Kamur. That timing would not impinge on church and family celebrations surrounding Christmas and would provide a convenient opportunity to gather the Sawi MAST facilitators and church leaders from all the surrounding Sawi villages for continued work on their Old Testament translation.

Working back from our planned arrival in Kamur on Saturday, January 5, allowing for additional meetings with

Papuan church leaders while transiting Jayapura, and considering airline schedules led us to a December 31 departure. Jan and I traveled with only carry-on baggage to avoid the potential for lost luggage on the multiple airline connections. We departed Orlando at 6 p.m. on Monday, New Year's Eve, and landed 46 hours later at 6 a.m. local time Thursday morning, January 3, in Jayapura, Papua, Indonesia.

It was good to be back in Papua. The last time I had been there was 21 years earlier when I flew a single-engine Cessna Caravan from California to Indonesia for Mission Aviation Fellowship.

Meeting Papuan Church Leaders

My former flight student, and MAF Papua program manager, Mike Brown, met us upon arrival. The Browns conveniently live across the street from the airport. We caught up with our friends over a home-cooked breakfast and refreshed for the day ahead.

By mid-morning Christov arrived with three Papuan pastors who wanted to talk about Bible translation needs within their church circles. Pastor William was part of the Indonesia Christian Church, formed through the evangelistic and church planting ministry of the Dutch Reformed Church. Pastor Hans was from the Pentecostal Church in Indonesia, affiliated internationally with the Foursquare Gospel Church. Pastor Yan was from a different affiliation of Reformed churches. As in my previous visits to Indonesia, it was encouraging to see the fruit of missionary work from churches of my Dutch heritage. Our Papua team had done tremendous work introducing MAST to these leaders and building a foundation for collaboration in Bible translation throughout their denominations.

After learning of the Bible translation progress made by the Sawi, Pastor William had hosted a MAST New Testament translation workshop in December 2018 for three language groups in the northern region of Papua. He had seen the

Bible translation progress and effectiveness firsthand and had already identified 16 more languages in their church areas eager to begin their translations.

The three Papuan pastors described the lack of Scripture in local languages as the greatest impediment to ongoing discipleship in their congregations. Scripture misunderstanding is common when the people are without a reference in their own language. They described an unhealthy dependence of the laity upon the clergy after decades of church growth in their denominations. They felt that further spiritual transformation would be achieved only if church members had ready access to Scripture in their heart language and learned to feed themselves from the meat of the Word. As they spoke, I couldn't help but think of the parallels between the Protestant Reformation and their description of Papua today. It is tragic that more than 500 years after the Reformation, Christians in Papua are still without God's Word in their own languages.

The pastors noted numerous secular programs at work to preserve local Papuan cultures and languages but said that from their perspective these were useless efforts. Pastor William said, "It's useless to preserve a culture bent on self-destruction without Christ. The gospel preserves cultural identity and glorifies God!" All three of these denominations have affiliate churches in remote rural areas of Papua. Their passion and commitment to strengthen these congregations and reach the surrounding tribes through Bible translation was contagious!

Their greatest concern as they committed to moving forward with Bible translation was for Biblical accuracy. They knew this was their greatest responsibility. So, we talked about the eight steps of MAST, the importance of involving church leadership in the strategy, and the references and tools already available in Indonesian and Papuan Malay that they could use during the translation process. They were especially grateful that these resources would be directly in the hands of local Papuan church leaders throughout their translation projects.

With three denominations represented at the table, it was inevitable that sensitivities about collaboration would surface. Pastor Hans summarized, "Dogma divides. Scripture unites!" As church leaders together, they agreed that opening access to Scripture for every language in Papua is more important than guarding their denominational boundaries. Many Papuan languages have multiple Christian denominations. Collaborating in Bible translation provides a tangible way to demonstrate unity within the body of Christ.

We closed our time together with prayer for one another and the declaration of our dependence upon God for His guidance and provision for the task ahead. It was an exciting glimpse into the future of Bible translation through the church in Papua.

Meeting Our Team

After a refreshing night of sleep in our temporary time zone, Jan and I were excited to have time together with our Papuan teammates in preparation for our time with the Sawi. Although Christov and Yanti had been part of our Papua team for some time, this was my first opportunity to meet them in person. They were already working closely with other members of our Indonesia and Asia teams but previously had contact with me only via email. We described our respective backgrounds and unique paths to involvement in Bible translation. I soon understood firsthand their well-deserved reputations as effective leaders.

After getting to know one another personally, we reviewed our engagement with the Sawi church and their progress thus far. Communications to remote Kamur are unpredictable at best. We understood that the Sawi church teams had continued to make progress on translation since the October workshop, but specifics were unclear. Most of the Sawi MAST facilitators planned to meet in Kamur during the coming week to make additional focused progress on their work. We would soon see what they had accomplished during November and December.

Christov and Yanti introduced me to my Papuan interpreter, Wesly. He had joined our Papua team after the October workshop, so this would be his first time in Kamur as well. Christov would stay in Sentani while we traveled, but two other colleagues, Sandy and Aldy, would join us to provide computer support for the Sawi teams.

Flying to the Swamp

Most MAF flights in Papua occur early in the morning before winds and weather gain strength. The flight from Sentani to Kamur would be just under two hours' duration, covering 250 miles and crossing the central mountain range with peaks above 12,000 feet in elevation. With no radio contact in Kamur to give us current weather reports, we depended on two things for weather information: 1) what we could see through the windshield, and 2) the weather notation on the bottom of the MAF approach chart for Kamur. The note said, "Weather Patterns: Typical South Coast. Low ceilings and morning fog common, improving throughout the day. Occasional isolated rain showers in the afternoon during west wind season (November—March)." In summary: likely fog, possible rain, definite mountains—just a typical day for MAF pilots in Papua. I was confident that Mike Brown, with 20 years of accident-free experience flying in Papua, was up to the task. We loaded our team of six passengers and baggage and departed for Kamur.

Because of my 15 years' serving with MAF, I know many places and pilots in Papua. As our plane ascended, heading southwest, I followed along on the map correlating the names and places to the landmarks along our route. Mike added color commentary over the headset to fill in additional history and geography. Our route took us just east of two places Jan and I had previously visited in Papua, Wamena and Bokondini. These villages are MAF bases for flights in the mountainous highlands of central Papua. Despite the early morning hour, many mountain peaks and ridge-lines were obscured by clouds. For safety, Mike altered our course further west and climbed high enough to assure plenty of clearance above the nearest peaks. As we crossed the ridges, the rainforest fell away steeply into the southern coastal swamp. Descending toward Kamur, it seemed the trees were exhaling the clouds from their canopy. Arriving from the north, we caught only a brief glimpse of the Kamur airstrip as we passed overhead the first time. Mike circled to the southwest and as we turned back toward Kamur, a gap in the clouds led us directly to the runway.

The place and people I had only imagined for over 40 years were now before my eyes.

Welcome

As we exited the plane, a crowd of Sawi welcomed us with shouts and embraces. They crowned me with emu feathers and gave Jan a traditional *noken* bag. Yanti and Sandy refreshed the friendships that had begun in October. Wesly and Aldy took in the Sawi sights and sounds for the first time. The crowd steered us down 'Main Street' toward Thomas and Rini's riverfront home. As the newest foreigners in town, we attracted quite a crowd. For many Sawi, watching us was their Saturday afternoon pastime. They filled the porch and lined the dock talking quietly—we assumed about us.

Rini served lunch for our team and several of the Sawi on the porch. At that point it was impossible to discern the unwritten rules for local hospitality. With my notepad at the ready and my interest piqued, I got the impression that the Sawi felt I might need time to recover from traveling. They were trying to let me relax when what I really wanted was to engage them immediately. With no specific agenda on our Saturday afternoon schedule, I simply opened a conversation with Wesly as my interpreter.

Before traveling to Kamur, I had spent a lot of time studying the *Peace Child* book. As I read it, I took note of every person named, which village they were from, and their parents' and grandparents' names. It was a complex task as Don had introduced more than 90 people in the book. I drew a diagram outlining all these relationships to begin understanding the Sawi community. I studied the diagram during the flights to Indonesia to have the names fresh in my mind.

As the unscripted conversation unfolded, I was alert to catch any mention of a familiar name. The names I recognized first were a few of the Sawi villages: Kamur, Haenam, Yohwi, and Seremeet. I learned that Haenam is hidden in the jungle just across the Kronkel River from Thomas and Rini's porch. The languid flow of the river set the pace for the afternoon. The conversation drifted toward some of the Sawi elders who had been close to Don. Many had died but their children and grandchildren were still alive. Others survived and continued to hold places of high esteem within the Sawi communities. Two of the remaining elders, Amhwi and Mavo, were frequently mentioned in the porch stories. Yohannes, the sole surviving peace child, was described as a community leader as well.

Torrential late-afternoon storms darkened the horizon in every direction and thinned the porch crowd. Raindrops fell with such size and speed that they seemed to bounce off the surface of the river before joining the current. The sheer volume of water falling from the sky was incalculable. I was just beginning to get a glimpse of how significantly water shapes the Sawi world.

Sunday

The rainfall stopped during the night but had noticeably widened the Kronkel River as it drained hundreds of square miles of watershed upstream. The water line on the pier was obviously higher and the previous day's riverbanks were clearly under water. The climbing sun heated the air so it could absorb still more humidity.

We gathered with the Sawi at Kalvari Church for Sunday worship. They seated us in the front of the congregation, graciously overlooking that Jan sat with me on the men's side of the church. The congregation overflowed from the chairs and benches onto the floor. Guitars set the tune and rhythm for singing. We were encouraged to hear a mixture of both recognizable and unrecognizable tunes. Familiar melodies affirmed the Sawi's vital connection to the global and historical church, and the native harmonies declared the Holy Spirit's vitality within the local church.

They invited me to provide an exhortation to the congregation. Standing before the Sawi community was a humbling and sobering experience. As had occurred when I was with Don, I felt I was trespassing on holy ground—the rightful domain of others. I could only lean on God's Word to speak appropriately.

I turned to one of my favorite passages—Isaiah 55:8-11:

> "For my thoughts are not your thoughts, neither are your ways my ways," declares the Lord. "As the heavens are higher than the earth, so are my ways higher than your ways and my thoughts than your thoughts. As the rain and the snow come down from heaven and do not return to it without watering the earth and making it bud and flourish, so that it yields seed for the sower and bread for the eater, so is my word that goes out from my mouth: it will not return to me empty, but will accomplish what I desire and achieve the purpose for which I sent it."

I noted that this passage is from the Old Testament, from a book that they had not yet begun to translate, but still God's voice they would recognize. They immediately grasped the opening statements of the difference in God's ways and thoughts. Although they've never seen snow in Kamur, many of the Sawi have seen it while traveling in the mountainous highlands. Naturally they have a thorough understanding of rain and the fruit it produces in the surrounding rainforest.

They had begun translating the Old Testament with fear and trembling, recognizing the sober responsibility they faced. Only faith moved them forward. So, to hear that God Himself sovereignly ordains the impact of His Word was deeply reassuring to them—as it is to me. In a small way, my exhortation helped them recalibrate their role in God's work. God gave His Old and New Testaments to accomplish His purposes. He invited the Sawi to be stewards of His Word, instruments in His hand, to impact all Sawi people. Theirs is an important stewardship, but the power is His alone.

Pastor Paulus followed with his own reflections and exhortations from Scripture. The mood was celebratory. Spiritual transformation that God had initiated through Don's ministry was continuing through the power of the Holy Spirit. More singing and shouts of "hallelujah" and "amen" filled the air. How exciting to witness their worship, knowing it was not dependent on outside support or influence but overflowed naturally from their tender and repentant hearts! It was beautiful!

Sawi Church Leaders

Following the morning worship service, about 20 Sawi church leaders gathered chairs together at the sagging corner of the auditorium. Several had worn their best Sunday suits despite the heat. All were barefoot in respect for the sanctuary. We circled together and began personal introductions.

They first introduced Pastor Amhwi. He had been the second Sawi to become a Christian and had been a primary leader in the Sawi church for more than 50 years. I rose to shake his hand while Wesly interpreted my greetings. "I remember that your parents were Amau and Manum, and that your children are Matius and Ribka," I ventured. He smiled and grasped both of my hands tightly. He introduced Matius seated nearby and Ribka smiling with the women on the other side of the room.

Next the leaders introduced Mavo, who was the Richardsons' house helper and the first Sawi to profess faith in Christ. He helped Don translate the Sawi New Testament and was an evangelist and pastor alongside Amhwi. "Your father was Taeri," I noted. Mavo smiled broadly through broken teeth.

The pastors wanted me to know that two other important Sawi leaders, Isai and Toh, had died in years past but their children were present. Isai was the young lookout who spotted Don through the trees on his first visit to Kamur. Isai later became a war leader for the Sawi. The pastors introduced me to Isai's daughter Natalia. I knew that Isai would have been about my age and I guessed that Natalia is about the same age as my oldest daughter, Abby. Natalia's face glowed with joy. She clearly picked up on my attempts to confirm family relationships. "Hadi was my grandfather," she offered. Hadi was Don's first interpreter to communicate with the Sawi. I later learned that Hadi was actually Natalia's grandmother's brother, but she called him "grandfather" because of their close relationship.

Sawi Church History

I asked the leaders to tell me how God had formed and strengthened the Sawi church from the beginning until now.

"We came close to God through Don," Amhwi said succinctly. What a simple, yet profound, statement. For generations past, God was distant. Don led them toward God, so now they are close to Him.

"The Sawi people responded immediately. We burned all of our weapons and amulets," Amhwi continued.

"Weren't you afraid that you would be defenseless against your enemies?" I asked.

"No. We knew that God was more powerful than our weapons and He would protect us," Amhwi said.

I was shocked by the simple way he described the dramatic change they had made from an aggressive warrior culture built on hatred, deception, and occult spiritual practices to a community of faith and peace. It was an outward reflection of their inward repentance—intentionally turning away from their past. Only 10 minutes into our first conversation, I was already beginning to sense the depth and breadth of God's work among them. *Peace Child* was clearly not the end of their story—it was merely the beginning.

Other church leaders began to add their perspectives as I balanced listening and taking notes. They described the first Sawi church as just a traditional house in Kamur. As more and more people turned to Christ, they built the "church on the ground" or "land church" as others called it. They described it as a thatched canopy with no walls or floor so they could squeeze more people in. Sawi Christians in other villages also began meeting in homes. Soon there were house churches in Yohwi, Seremeet, and Kagas.

The number of Sawi Christians increased as Don, Amhwi, Mavo, Isai, Narai, and Toh traveled to every Sawi village to tell them of God's peace child—Jesus Christ. Don also formed a Bible school to translate and teach them the New Testament. These five leaders were joined by another seven Sawi men for Bible training.

Help From the Highlands

Christian missionaries were bringing the gospel to the Dani tribe living in the central Papuan mountain region just a few years prior to the Richardsons' arrival in Kamur. After Dani tribesmen turned to Christ, they soon began reaching out to other Papuan tribes with the gospel. When word spread throughout Papua that the violent Sawi had made peace, the Dani responded by sending their own missionaries.

The Sawi recalled that the Dani missionaries included evangelists, pastors, nurses, teachers, and builders. Nanggen, Wanduak, Yanawandik, Mayus, Bunggen, Ami, Obet, and Yusuf, along with their families, lived among the Sawi for many years. They learned the Sawi language and, as brothers and sisters in Christ, encouraged the Sawi in their faith.

The Dani stayed with the Sawi long after the Richardson and Mills families had departed. The Dani invited 12 younger Sawi church leaders to attend Bible school in their highland village of Bokondini.

Over the years the Sawi built 15 churches to serve their villages. The Sawi body of Christ now exceeds 10,000 Christians from three generations. Pastor Amhwi baptized many of them himself. Together Sawi and Dani missionaries evangelized the surrounding Asmat, Atohwaem, Auyu, and Kayagar tribes. These neighboring tribes no longer view the Sawi as their mortal enemies but as their spiritual fathers, brothers, and sisters.

Church Challenges

After hearing the stories of God's providential care and equipping of the Sawi church, I asked the leaders what challenges they are currently facing. Some are theological. Islam continues to migrate into their community slowly, one family at a time. But Sawi church leaders have limited the Muslims to a single mosque and are effectively resisting Muslim efforts to convert Sawi to Islam by countering with sound Biblical teaching. Pentecostal theology has raised questions about spiritual gifts and miracles that the Sawi leaders are answering from Scripture. The Sawi see their Old Testament translation as an essential resource for equipping the local people with sharpened spiritual discernment for the days ahead.

The Sawi church also faces physical challenges. Their classis of 15 churches has no central office or staff. Domingus is the elected head of the classis but has limited resources to support his care for the churches. The only practical way to reach all the Sawi communities is by boat. But since the classis owns neither a boat nor motor, the pastors often pay for transportation from their own pockets.

Interviews and Resumes

Our Sunday afternoon group conversation gave me a great overview of the trends and dynamics of the Sawi church over the past 50 years. In the days that followed, I had private conversations with each church leader, several translators who participated in the October MAST workshop and ongoing translation work, and government leaders in Kamur and Haenam villages. Together these conversations painted a detailed picture of God powerfully at work in and through the Sawi church.

Every Sawi pastor personally participated in the Old Testament translation workshop. Some had continuing responsibilities as translation team leaders while others served within those teams. Of the 14 Sawi translation team leaders, 8 had university degrees and 2 were in degree programs including theology, Christian education, public administration, and science. They ranged in age from 22 to 64. All of them spoke Sawi as their first language—their heart language.

Local Perspective

Without exception all Sawi Christians with whom I spoke said they had been praying and hoping for the Old Testament ever since they received the New Testament. Yanti didn't persuade them it was necessary. She merely told them it was possible, and they stepped up to the challenge immediately. Despite their longstanding eagerness for the Old Testament, they were uncertain they would be up to the task of translation. They had never considered the possibility of translating it themselves, nor had they heard of any other Papuan people translating Scripture. The concept was new and daunting, but it piqued their interest.

After experiencing the MAST workshop in October, they were THRILLED! They sensed the movement of the Holy Spirit inspiring and empowering them for the work. With 211 Sawi working together, they realized how God had prepared them to be stewards of His Word. Completing translation of 15 books in 8-1/2 days showed them what was possible.

While I was interviewing individuals, the rest of the translators were hard at work. The small translation groups had made further progress during November but were preoccupied with Christmas celebrations during December. My January visit became an opportunity for them to consolidate their progress and prepare for the next season of translation.

During the week I visited, they continued working on the 7 Old Testament books started in October, and assigned the remaining 17 books to the church teams. Their consensus was that they would certainly finish translating the Old Testament in less than one year.

Overlooked

While I was in Kamur, pastors from two neighboring language groups asked to speak with me. The conversations were heartbreaking.

Pastor Nehemiah is from the Kayagar tribe. Although he was born a few years after the Richardsons moved to Kamur, he grew up hearing the story of Don's passage through the Kayagar territory. Don had initially met up with established RBMU missionaries in the Kayagar village of Kawem to prepare for his onward journey. It was there that Don hired three Kayagar paddlers to take him upstream into the Sawi domain. It was Kayagar courage and sweat that enabled Don to reach the Sawi the first time. Along the way the Kayagar made multiple attempts to dissuade Don from continuing, inviting him to settle with them instead. But Don insisted they honor their agreement to take him all the way to the Sawi.

In the years that followed, Nehemiah's childhood years, the Kayagar responded to the missionaries' preaching of the gospel. It was truly good news for them, having lived in a similar context of violence and spiritism as the Sawi. When the Kayagar heard that the Sawi had abandoned violence and chosen peace, they celebrated. When the New Testament was translated into Sawi, the Kayagar rejoiced with them.

"Why doesn't anyone care about us?" Pastor Nehemiah's tears became my own. "We had missionaries. We have the gospel. But we don't have any Scripture. Why didn't our missionaries translate the Bible for us?" It was an impossible question for me, but one that demanded an answer.

I didn't know the missionaries who went to the Kayagar. I asked Nehemiah what he had seen the missionaries do while they were there. The missionaries learned their language and obviously had preached the gospel. Nehemiah described a medical clinic the missionaries had established. But eventually the missionaries moved on and the Kayagar were left alone—without Scripture. Nehemiah recognized the temporary blessings of having missionaries in his community but lived his entire life yearning for God's Word in his own language.

Nehemiah was "accidentally" in Kamur the September day when Yanti arrived to meet the Sawi. Nehemiah listened to the description of training the Sawi to translate their Old Testament and the question deep in his heart surfaced. "Why doesn't anyone care about us?" He decided the best thing he could do was to return in October to learn what the Sawi would learn. But when he returned, he found himself struggling to understand MAST—because he doesn't speak Sawi. He understood the instructions in Indonesian but struggled to apply them to Kayagar. His frustration deepened.

When I arrived in Kamur, one of Nehemiah's friends, a Kayagar man married to a Sawi woman, called him to tell him he should speak to me. "We need the Bible in Kayagar. We have seven churches, more than 20,000 people in 19 villages, and we are ready to do the work. Will you help us?" Nehemiah pled. I replied, "There are two ways you can get the Bible. You can get help from far away, or you can get help close by. Which do you think would be better?" The answer was obvious: "Close by."

The second pastor to approach me was Pastor Yohannes from the Atohwaem people. He was 10 years younger than Nehemiah but had heard about Don Richardson from Hadi, his uncle. When Don first arrived in Kamur, Hadi was his multilingual interpreter. Pastor Yohannes was at the November meeting of the Gospel Churches of Indonesia in Bokondini, where he heard the Sawi pastors report on their recent progress in Bible translation. When he told this news to the Atohwaem church leaders back home, they charged him to find out how they could begin translating Scripture. News of my arrival somehow reached him, so he came to find me. "My uncle helped Don Richardson reach the Sawi. We have six villages and many Christians. We have young people who know how to use computers. We are ready. Please teach us how to translate Scripture. We need the Bible in Atohwaem."

Fortunately for me, the Sawi church leaders had already offered to assist both the Kayagar and Atohwaem with their translations. Kalvari Church in Kamur is the largest church building in the entire region, and the Sawi leaders invited Nehemiah and Yohannes to bring their people to Kamur to learn MAST. Naturally, our Wycliffe Associates team offered to train and equip their translators as well. Before I left Kamur, two more nearby language groups, Kombai and Asmat, had contacted the Sawi asking to join the next Bible translation workshop. Word was getting out.

Wildlife

Sandy and Aldy worked with the Sawi translators all week to update their translation files and print copies of the most recently completed Old Testament books. The work often occupied them until late at night. Jan and I frequently retired for the evening immediately following Rini's dinner. The mosquito net over our bed reduced our workload fending off wildlife.

The rest of our team overlapped working and sleeping in the main living room. One night we were all awakened by screaming and scuffling when a rat scurried across the living room sleepers. Another night Sandy had to be awakened by Wesly from a violent nightmare. Sandy was writhing and coughing as he dreamed a wolf pounced on his chest. Wesly rebuked the spirit in Jesus' name and Sandy was immediately released from the attack.

After a week interviewing Sawi leaders in and around Kalvari Church, I learned that one of the men had killed a poisonous Sawi snake—the kind they feared had bitten the small child in October—by a small wooden platform I had employed to minimize disruption to the ongoing translation work.

Clearly, we don't always know what threats will surface as we clear the path for God's Word to reach every tribe and tongue.

Farewell

Every day we were in Kamur, it rained heavily. Sometimes the rain gathered in the late afternoon. Other days the torrent fell in the middle of the night and continued through morning. We often enjoyed sitting on Thomas and Rini's porch watching the rain pelt the surface of the Kronkel River and give new meaning to the rainforest on the opposite bank. Day by day we could see the cumulative result of the rains as the Kronkel rose higher and wider. In the low-lying swamp, a river loses its boundaries and fills every available space. At one point I tried to imagine how many cubic feet of water had to fall for the river to rise a single inch. It was beyond my imagination, but it was not imaginary. During the week we were in Kamur, the Kronkel River rose at least two feet! On Friday the public pier just upstream was completely submerged, and Thomas' pier was within inches of the same plight. As the rain continued falling, on Friday morning I wondered whether Mike might have difficulty getting into Kamur. The treetops were again exhaling fog.

By faith we began walking the half mile from our hostel to the airport. All appeared well until we reached the airport entry gate. The path to the airport terminal was under two feet of water! As we reluctantly pondered wading or swimming, an enterprising Sawi quickly grasped the solution. He disappeared down the road and returned a few minutes later paddling his canoe up the drainage ditch. He then ferried us two at a time for the 50 yards across the flooded yard to the airport terminal steps. That was the first time I have ever taken a canoe to an airport terminal.

I heard the MAF plane fly overhead but couldn't see it through the clouds. As the noise of the engine faded to the south, I studied the ends of the runway imagining what Mike might see from the cockpit. The clouds seemed impenetrable to the west. To the east they seemed a bit more broken. Without a radio there was no way for me to get word to Mike. But a moment later I spotted him approaching from the southeast. He touched down gently and taxied up to his waiting passengers and Sawi onlookers.

A few short minutes later, we departed to the east. The clouds had lifted and broken a bit more, so we had a good view of Kamur as we turned north toward Sentani. I often wonder how I can survive leaving a piece of my heart in every village I visit. A big piece of my heart certainly remains with the Sawi.

14

Pressing Forward

Meanwhile in the Jungle

During the early months of 2019, as the Sawi Bible translation teams worked in their villages, numerous challenges surfaced.

First, there was the normal challenge of survival. The jungle doesn't deliver, so hunting and gathering food is normally a full-time job. The community and extended family can cover these provisions for individuals temporarily; but eventually, survival requires everyone's time and energy.

Second, there was the new challenge of caring for computer tablets in a hostile environment. Some of the tablets succumbed to the tropical heat, the pervasive 100 percent humidity, or the invasion of foraging insects. Other tablets were inadvertently electrocuted by unregulated generator current. Some digitized translation was lost; but fortunately, most of it was also on paper. The surviving tablets became the vital channel into which paper and pen translations were funneled. But the Sawi pressed on.

The Cell Phone Story

When I visited Papua in January 2019, they told me a joke that was circulating there about cell phones.

A Papuan went to a store and bought a cell phone so he could talk to his friends. To his dismay, no matter how he tried he couldn't figure out how to make it work. When he returned to the store to complain, the manager explained, "Now you have to buy the cell signal."

For Papuans, this is more than a joke about cell phones. It is the story of how outsiders routinely take advantage of them and how real solutions often remain just out of reach.

For several months it was impossible for our Papuan MAST team to communicate with the Sawi. When contact was finally made with individuals we were able to get only fragmented reports from some of the translation teams. We knew that all the books and chapters of the Old Testament had been assigned to the church teams, but their translation progress was unknown.

How do you feel when you are unable to communicate with someone you care about? It is easy, but seldom productive, to fill the void with speculation. Instead of doing that, I filled the time with prayer. The Sawi got along quite well without my help for a lot of years. They have the Holy Spirit. They have church leaders, experience, the New Testament in Sawi, and the Old Testament in Indonesian. The Sawi don't work for me. They don't owe me reports or progress. God has fully equipped them to steward His Word. It was a time for me to simply watch, listen, and pray.

Signs of Progress

Word eventually came from Yakobus and Ribka that during the spring the teams were working on Genesis, Exodus, Joshua, Judges, 1 and 2 Kings, 2 Chronicles, Job, Psalms, Hosea, and Ezekiel. Together these books are a major percentage of the Old Testament, and the Old Testament is three times the length of the New Testament. So, it was encouraging to hear of their progress.

During a gap in our communications with the Sawi, I noticed that a MAST workshop appeared on our June 2019 planning calendar for the Kombai language in Papua. It caught my eye because I had met a Kombai man named Kambuwop, who is married to the Sawi translator Natalia. His story stuck in my mind for two reasons. First, he described growing up in the village of Boven Digoel—a former Dutch prison camp. The Dutch had chosen that location because its extreme isolation and the surrounding violent tribes discouraged prisoners from escaping. Second, the Kombai and neighboring tribes had become an international curiosity in recent years when journalists discovered they continued to live in houses built among the treetops. The Sawi built homes like this before Don showed them how to drive pilings into the swamp.

Kambuwop didn't ask me for help teaching the Kombai to do Bible translation. He had participated in the October Sawi MAST workshop and was already recruiting his Sawi friends to go to Boven Digoel with him to launch their New Testament translation. The Kombai started translating their New Testament on June 3, 2019. He has also been spreading the word about MAST within the Reformed Churches of Papua and has a list of 19 more languages in south Papua that want to begin Bible translation as soon as possible.

A few weeks later I saw MAST workshops for the Atohwaem and Kayagar languages appear on our August planning calendar—and the location listed Kamur. I was THRILLED! Clearly, the Sawi were not keeping what they'd learned to themselves. They were reaching out to the neighboring tribes even as they continued their Old Testament translation. In early August I heard that 17 members of our Papua MAST team were planning to return to Kamur to assist with the workshop since the three language groups were planning to send 30 translators each. The interpreter from my January visit, Wesly, would be leading the workshop this time.

A Dark and Stormy Night

Once the dates were set, Wesly went to the MAF hangar in Sentani to schedule the Kamur flights for the MAST facilitation team. Unfortunately, MAF was unable to schedule these flights due to missionary pilot furloughs. They referred him to Yajasi, another missionary flight organization; but he again came away with no solutions. After conferring with Yanti, and recalling her difficulty finding anyone in Merauke that knew how to get to Kamur, they decided to take a commercial flight from Sentani to Timika and continue to Kamur by boat.

Straight line distance from Timika to Kamur is 170 miles. In a small plane, this would take about one hour of flight time. However, by boat, the distance is more than 220 miles—including more than 150 miles on the open ocean. At an average speed of 10 knots, they anticipated a journey of 22 hours in a 24-foot longboat.

The longboat captain and crew of two men had never made the trip to Kamur before, but they knew the ocean and the rivers. The best time to travel in order to escape the relentless sun and heat was at night. Our team of 17 boarded the boat in Timika at 1 a.m. on Friday, August 16. The captain turned the boat downstream, headed out to the Arafura Sea on the south coast of Papua.

Within the first half-hour, it began to rain—not just a light shower, but a pelting tropical storm. The women huddled under a small cover with the captain at the back of the boat. The men laid on the bottom of the boat, fruitlessly attempting to fend off the driving rain. The urge to turn back was overcome by the hope that the rain would end and the deep conviction of the importance of their mission. Within a few hours, the river emptied into the sea. The rain didn't let up, and the ocean waves increased everyone's discomfort. Around 7 a.m. one passenger fainted, and another was swooning. Soon thereafter the first passenger began vomiting, then the second, then the third—Wesly.

Wesly later wrote, "If it was not because of the favor of God, we did not know what would happen with our lives. Since we faced heavy rain on the sea, my prayer to God was asking God to protect all of the team members and to strengthen their faith despite the rain and waves."

By the time the storm passed, everyone on the boat was exhausted—but they still had 18 hours' journey to reach Kamur. To push the longboat through the waves and avoid capsizing, the captain was running all three outboard motors. The motors were consuming fuel at an alarming rate leaving everyone, including the captain, wondering when they would give out.

After an agonizing night and day at sea churning in the belly of a tropical storm, they turned onto the Kronkel River just before sunset. They soon came to a village where they were able to walk on solid ground, take care of biological needs, eat a bowl of hot noodles, and drink some coffee. Although the rain continued throughout the trip, they reboarded the longboat for the remaining journey. They reached the dock at Kamur at 1 a.m. on Saturday, August 17.

When they told the Sawi the story of their journey, the Sawi said that no one in their entire history had ever made the journey from Timika to Kamur in a longboat. When Wesly told me this story, I said he was lucky the others didn't throw him overboard! He sent me the report in an email a couple days after their arrival, pleading for assistance in arranging their return flight to Sentani at the conclusion of the workshop. I reached out to my MAF U.S. contacts as Christov reached out to his MAF Indonesia contacts. Within a few hours, the return flight was booked—to the great comfort and relief of everyone involved.

August 2019 MAST Workshop

The workshop opened with 69 translators and 17 facilitators. Our Papuan computer technician began triage on the Sawi computer tablets. The Papuan facilitators met with the 28 Kayagar and 11 Atohwaem translators and began teaching them the eight steps of MAST. The two pastors I had met in January, Nehemiah and Yohannes, were there to lead their teams. The 30 Sawi translators knew what they had to do, so they continued their Old Testament translation assignments as the Kayagar and Atohwaem started their New Testaments.

On Tuesday 15 more Atohwaem translators arrived, temporarily increasing their numbers. But on Wednesday they received word of the death of an Atohwaem child back home, so several had to leave the MAST workshop to return to their extended families.

The Kayagar divided their 28 translators into three teams, tackling three of the gospels—Matthew, Mark, and John. While the Sawi had been praying 50 years for the Old Testament, the Kayagar were praying to have any Scripture at all in their heart language. As the gospels began to unfold through the eight steps of MAST, the Kayagar teams were overjoyed!

Because of their smaller, and changing, numbers of translators, the Atohwaem focused only on the gospel of Luke. The English translation of Luke is 1151 verses and 19,482 words, around 14 percent of the entire New Testament. So even with this limited focus, the Atohwaem translators were tackling a significant portion of their overall goal.

The Snake Rears His Ugly Head

One day as the translation teams were working, a young woman named Yuli collapsed to the floor moaning. Initially, it wasn't clear what had caused her to fall. But as others surrounded her, the consensus grew that she was experiencing a spiritual attack. Pastor Paulus discerned that the spirit of the Sawi snake was confronting Yuli and opposing the translation work. The Papuan MAST facilitators joined with the Sawi, Kayagar, and Atohwaem translators in prayer for God's protection and strength to overcome the demonic powers. Within moments, Yuli was recovering and returning to work.

Rather than discouraging the translators, as Satan intended, this attack strengthened the faith of everyone present. It reminded them of the importance of God's Word in the spiritual battle for the souls of their families and friends. It gave them a specific opportunity to thank God for empowering them for this work, and for the Holy Spirit's presence in them. As they translated Matthew 7, Mark 16, and Luke 9, they felt camaraderie with the disciples in the spiritual battle taking place throughout human history.

A few days later, one of the men killed a deadly Sawi snake as it slithered near the church.

The Workshop Conclusion

By the end of the two-week MAST workshop, despite the distractions, the Atohwaem translators completed drafting and checking the entire gospel of Luke. The Kayagar translators completed drafting and checking all of Matthew, 5 chapters of Mark, and 16 chapters of John. In addition, the 11 remaining chapters of Mark and 5 chapters of John were completely drafted and in the checking process. More important, the Atohwaem and Kayagar teams returned home experienced and equipped to continue the work to its conclusion. Both groups are praying and working to complete their New Testaments within a year and continue on to translating the Old Testament as well. They also know they are not forgotten or alone in their efforts. Their Sawi neighbors and the Papuan MAST team are ready, willing, and able to assist them in their efforts to get God's Word to all the Atohwaem and Kayagar people.

At this point, the Sawi translators had completed drafting and checking 22 Old Testament books, with 11 more books nearing completion. The six books with significant translation work remaining are 1 Samuel, 2 Kings, 1 Chronicles, Proverbs, Isaiah, and Jeremiah. For perspective, the Sawi had completed translating 671 chapters of the Old Testament—the equivalent of about 2-1/2 New Testaments—in 10 months. Their goal is to complete their Old Testament translation before the end of 2019.

The Journey Ahead

During the closing months of 2019, the Sawi are pressing toward their immediate goal of completing their Old Testament translation. But that isn't their final goal. Their ultimate goal is careful and continuous stewardship of God's Word for all people of Papua. For the Sawi this not only means completing their Old Testament, it means revising their New Testament. With great respect for the work that Don Richardson, John Mills, and the Sawi translation assistants did in their original New Testament translation, the Sawi believe it is time to revise the New Testament to speak with a native Sawi voice. They also describe five distinct Sawi dialects, each of which—in their view—needs its own Bible translations. They now have the experience, equipment, and allies to carefully steward God's Word for themselves. They also have the heart and vision to share their knowledge and experience with their neighbors throughout Papua.

Do They Speak Sawi?

In the days ahead, someone will hear that the Sawi have translated the Old Testament and may ask, "What makes you think you are qualified to translate the Bible into Sawi?" In anticipation of that future conversation, I posed this question to the Sawi church leaders and translators themselves. Their answers were enlightening.

"We are the Sawi. Everyone knows our history and reputation. They know the price we paid for peace among our people, and that God gave His *peace child* so we could have peace with Him. We once were few people and now are many. We have 15 churches and more than 10,000 Sawi Christians. We have been a witness and testimony to our neighbors near and far. We abandoned our weapons and fetishes. We repented of our evil ways. God in His great love spoke to us through His Word. We have studied and obeyed it for 50 years. We have the Holy Spirit to teach and correct us. Only a person who doesn't know us would ask this question. If we are not qualified to translate the Bible in our own language, then no one is."

In the western world, our lives can be very compartmentalized. For us family, faith, education, work, and recreation often coexist but may overlap only in limited ways. Our education is measured by formal degrees. The Sawi world is less compartmentalized—more integrated. Education doesn't only happen in school. It occurs through all of life, during a conversation while hunting in the jungle, while listening in on the elders as they discuss past generations, reflecting on the glorious testimony of creation while floating down the river in a canoe, and through trial and error experimentation with peers. These are the things that make the Sawi experts at being Sawi. Many Sawi now have formal education, but all Sawi have the rich vocabulary of a lifetime in their culture.

The Sawi select their own chief, their own community leaders, their own church leaders. They don't ask outsiders to approve their decisions. The Sawi church is self-governing, self-sustaining, and self-supporting. This is not to say that they are independent. They are interdependent. They are connected to neighboring communities and churches. They value these relationships but make their own decisions. They are adults, masters of their world, and the healthy body of Christ in their remote corner of Papua.

Considering all these things, I asked the Sawi leaders what they would say if someone came to them asking to check their translation. Independently, each of the leaders replied with exactly the same succinct response: "Do they speak Sawi?"

How Firm a Foundation

When Don arrived in Kamur in 1962, one of the first things he did was to build a house. At that time, the Sawi lived in houses built high in the trees. But Don built his house on ironwood pilings driven deep into the marshy soil. The Sawi had to search deep in the jungle to find ironwood. Driving the pilings deep into the soil took tremendous time and energy in the suffocating tropical heat. As the Sawi did this work for Don, they had no understanding of its importance. But Don understood.

A strong foundation stands the test of time.

I had the opportunity to visit the Richardsons' former home-site in Kamur. From the river, there is no evidence that a house ever stood on that ground. After 50 years the bush wood roof, walls, and floors are no more. Slowly but surely, the structure disintegrated. Heat and humidity boiled the sinew. Insects gutted the poles and beams until they sagged and fell away. Knotted vines stretched, then snapped. Rains and floods washed away the debris. Enterprising Sawi have lately redeemed the high ground for a small garden.

But when I walked through the garden, I saw that the iron-wood pilings are still in place. They are exactly where Don positioned them—as strong today, as ever.

> "How firm a foundation, ye saints of the Lord,
> is laid for your faith in His excellent Word!
> What more can He say than to you He hath
> said, who unto the Savior for refuge have fled?"
> John Rippon, 1787.

The Word of God is the foundation that every nation, tribe, people, and language needs.

15

BIBLE TRANSLATION TODAY

Counting Down or Counting Up?

I am in my twentieth year of full-time engagement in Bible translation. Throughout these years the total number of languages in the world as officially cataloged by linguistic researchers has fluctuated around 7,000. As research continues, the number rises or falls based on the changes in several variables that comprise the research definition of a language. But according to the Linguistic Society of America, there is "no such count that has any status as a scientific finding of modern linguistics." A quick Google search of "language definition" yielded 418 million hits in .44 seconds. Even accounting for significant overlapping definitions, this suggests there are many ways to look at languages. At Wycliffe Associates, we often find that the language communities themselves view their languages quite differently than foreign linguists do.

When Don Richardson learned the Sawi language, he understood it as a single language, differentiated from other nearby languages like Atohwaem, Kayagar, and Auyu. But as we spoke to the Sawi about their New Testament, they described it as a combination of two Sawi dialects. When the Sawi described their current need for Bible translation, they mentioned five Sawi dialects—each needing its own Bible translation. Don was surprised to hear all of this. From an external perspective, we might say that all five Sawi dialects could be adequately served by a single Bible translation. But from the internal Sawi church perspective, this is not the case.

Who decides how many Bible translations are needed?

For most minority people groups, the decision of whether a language needs Bible translation has been made by majority people groups. Perhaps you can imagine how this feels to speakers of minority languages.

Our Wycliffe Associates team faces these conflicting definitions of translation needs almost daily. In one location our team met with church leaders and showed them our list of seven languages in their area. They laughed, "It's actually 70 languages." On the opposite side of the world, in a totally different cultural context, we reviewed a list of 44 languages with the local church leaders. "These five are not languages—they are cities. And you are missing at least a dozen languages." The language research in this country had been done during a period of political instability more than 50 years ago and hadn't been updated since then.

Even in situations where the linguistic research is accurate, the determination of whether a language needs Scripture is a subjective decision. The very first people to pioneer MAST in South Asia were classified by Christian missions researchers as "unreached, unengaged, and no need for

Bible translation." But the Christians there disagreed; and by stepping forward in faith to translate Scripture, they opened a path for millions of Christians in other minority languages to decide for themselves whether they need Scripture.

Based on our conversations with church leaders around the globe, it appears that the number of Bible translations needed worldwide could be double or triple the western research estimates. Rather than attempting to apply an external definition or decision matrix to evaluate this number, we are simply proceeding to train and equip everyone we can to steward God's Word for themselves—and encouraging them to teach their neighbors to do this as well. By making Bible translation freely accessible to everyone in the world, we increasingly make any number of Bible translations achievable—and since these translations can be done simultaneously by the local churches, no one has to wait!

How Much Scripture is Enough?

Can you imagine a church leader, or any Christian for that matter, saying, "We don't need the Bible in our language"? Or how about, "We just want a few books, but not the whole Bible"? It might be easier to imagine someone saying, "We are very happy to have the New Testament, but we are okay without the Old Testament."

As of September 2019, our Wycliffe Associates team has had conversations with Christians in 2,651 languages. In all these conversations, no one has ever answered as I just described. No one.

When Yanti asked the Sawi, "Do you want the Old Testament?" Their immediate answer was, "OF COURSE!" In fact, they wanted the Old Testament long before we asked the question. This is typical of the way our conversations with church leaders have gone. They have been yearning for, and praying for, Scripture—the whole testimony of God, both Old and New—for years. When we ask if they want Scripture in their language, they don't say, "I don't know. We've never thought of that." Most often they say, "We assumed that no one cared enough to help us have Scripture." Or they say, "People have told us we don't deserve Scripture."

It's heartbreaking.

Does any Christian think that some people are better off without Scripture in their own language? Wycliffe Associates does not think so. I certainly don't think so.

In 34 years of international ministry, I've traveled to more than 100 countries. Within those countries, I've spoken, eaten, traveled, cried, and prayed with thousands of people. I've received the hospitality of people living in the most desperate poverty and hopelessness. I've been embraced by people whose only prior contact with an American has been through a gunsight. I've also seen the transformational impact God's Word makes when people in these circumstances have Scripture in their heart language. "For the Word of God is living and active. Sharper than any double-edged sword, it penetrates even to dividing soul and spirit, joints and marrow; it judges the thoughts and attitudes of the heart" (Hebrews 4:12). God's Word changes hearts—it's a verifiable fact.

No one is better off without Scripture in their language. They may get a glimpse of truth through Scripture in a foreign language. But as someone well said, "Hearing Scripture in a foreign language is like eating a banana without peeling it. Hearing Scripture in my heart language is like peeling the banana—it tastes much better." No one would prepare a banana dish with some bananas peeled and others unpeeled. In the same way, people need God's whole testimony translated—not just portions.

How Big is a Church?

Since at least the 1980s, Christian missions researchers have been using the phrase "unreached people groups" to describe people at the margins of Christianity globally. My first understanding of the meaning of this phrase was that it referred to ethnic groups with less than 2 percent Christians. It was a way to focus attention on the least-reached ethnic groups below this statistical threshold. My own practical experience with this definition includes connecting with unreached people groups with populations from as few as 300 to as many as 3 million. The math is simple but telling. A population of 3 million people could have 59,999 Christians and still be below the 2 percent threshold. A similar population of 300 people with just 5 Christians is also defined as unreached. But the practical difference between having 5 Christians versus 59,999 Christians is significant.

Other missionaries have experienced this same dynamic and have begun redefining what constitutes an "unreached people group." Again, a Google search on this phrase yielded 597,000 results in .46 seconds. My unscientific sampling of these results revealed lots of new variables that are being included in the equations used to calculate the Christian witness within ethnic groups. "Ethnic" is yet another term with multiple definitions.

At Wycliffe Associates, we are finding it helpful to simply accept the definition given by the local people. It is somewhat shocking to me that in the conversations we've had with 2,651 language groups we've found only one in which we have not yet met Christians. That's a very small percentage. You might notice I said, "Not yet." Based on the data set of 2,650 other languages, all of which have Christians, I assume that there are Christians in this one language whom we will soon meet. You might also notice I said, "somewhat shocking." After 2,650 conversations in which we have found Christians, I am no longer shocked by the pervasive global spread of Christianity. Christian missions worked— and is working. The number of language groups worldwide with no Christians is practically approaching zero.

Our approach to Bible translation is under the authority of the local church. We don't tell churches what to do. We ask them how we can serve them. We can't meet all their needs, but we can help them steward God's Word for their people. As we engage in these conversations, we've had to wrestle with the definition of "church."

It has been helpful for us to consider the biblical definition of "church." You can research the Greek or Hebrew equivalents as easily as I can, but you may find them less helpful than you hope. Matthew 18:20 says, "For where two or three come together in my name, there I am with them." As far as I can tell, this is the only quantitative biblical reference that informs our understanding of a church—more than one person. In 1 Corinthians 12 Paul describes "the body of Christ" qualitatively at some length and detail.

One language group we've met tells us there are only three living speakers of their language—all of whom are Christians. Do these three Christians constitute the church in their language group? I would say they do. When these three Christians asked for training to translate the Bible into their language how should we have responded? One reasonable response would be that these are too few people and too brief a benefit for our investment of resources. That is not how we responded. Instead, we invited them to attend a MAST workshop for training along with several other languages. The incremental cost of including them in this workshop was very small. But to these three Christians, it was priceless.

Many language groups have multiple churches. Which of these constitute the local church? This is a question we pose to Christians when we meet them. In our view, only they can pragmatically answer this question. The church variations in local groups seem to be equal to or greater in number than the number of languages themselves. As the local conversation about Bible translation expands, some churches align while other churches choose to distance themselves. Some churches prefer to conduct worship and Bible reading in majority languages while others reject the majority language Bible translation for various reasons. We encourage the local Christians to pray and seek God's guidance on who to invite to participate in Bible translation. On most occasions, this builds a Bible translation team that is a thorough representation of the body of Christ in their community. On a few occasions, local Christians have followed God's guidance to invite non-Christians to participate in the translation. I will say that this has been uncomfortable for me, but I have seen the wisdom of the local churches' decisions. In several cases, the non-Christians became Christians while translating Scripture. MAST workshops have been "interrupted" by baptisms. Even in situations where the non-Christians did not immediately become Christians, the Bible translation has gained an audience and credibility among non-Christians because of their participation. I not only believe Isaiah 55:9 when it says, "As the heavens are higher than the earth, so are my ways higher than your ways and my thoughts than your thoughts," I have seen it to be true repeatedly. I have also seen the judgment of local Christians to be consistently better than my own judgment. As a result, I've learned to prefer their judgment.

Data Points and Trends

As of this writing, around 700 languages have the entire Bible. Of the 2,651 language groups with whom we've spoken, 1,290 have used MAST to begin translating the New Testament during the past 5 years. Of these languages, 237 have already completed their New Testament. Another 112 languages have used MAST to start translating their Old Testament, with 25 already completed.

I don't know whether these numbers sound high or low to you. To me they are miraculous. To the best of our knowledge, this reflects the greatest advance of Bible translation into new languages of any similar season in world history! Praise God from Whom all blessings flow!

At the same time, I remain obsessed with concern for all the languages still without a single verse of Scripture. If we've had conversations with 2,651 language groups, why have only 1,402 started their translations? The amazing news is that 359 more of these languages are planning to begin Bible translation within the next few months! We are also in active discussion with 382 more of these languages to set a start date for their translations to begin.

At What Cost?

As MAST unfolded, we initially found that our direct costs for each workshop were averaging around $19,500. Several language groups brought more than 25 translators to their MAST workshop and completed drafting and checking their entire New Testament during a single workshop! Many language groups recruited three to five translators to attend the MAST workshop and planned to complete their New Testament translation in two to four years. We've also seen that as we increasingly ask the local people to make the planning decisions regarding MAST workshops—the cost is plummeting! As insiders, they have networks, relationships, resources, and creativity that they leverage for greater economy. This kind of stewardship is increasingly multiplying the impact of our support.

Great Commission Bible Translation

As MAST gained momentum among hundreds of languages, we realized that as long as it depended on Wycliffe Associates' resources, its reach would be limited. The only way to scale its benefits globally is to get it into the hands of the global church. To do this we launched a two-pronged strategy.

To begin engaging the global church, we invited 20 church leaders from the 13 countries with the largest number of languages still without Scripture to meet for the first Great Commission Bible Translation (GCBT) conference in Manila in November 2017. The premise was simple but profound. We affirmed their leadership and authority within their churches and invited them to consider the place of Bible translation within their churches' priorities. We introduced the MAST process, reported on its progress, gave them a firsthand experience to see how it works in their own languages, and offered to serve them as they judge best.

The impact was significant. The best way to describe the impact is in their own words. Those 20 church leaders drafted what has come to be known within our circles as the Manila Declaration. The complete text follows:

> We, the delegates of the Great Commission Bible Translation conference, Manila, 16 November 2017, representing the countries of Africa, Asia-Pacific, and the United States of America, after having prayed, discussed, and deliberated: freely and wholeheartedly, affirm and commit ourselves to the following statements and affix our signatures.
>
> 1. We affirm the call of Jesus Christ to take the Good News to every people group in our various countries and around the world. In this light, we are committed to serve and support the local churches in their responsibility to provide God's Word to their people in their heart language.
>
> 2. We affirm that the translation of God's Word in all the languages of the world in various forms—written, audio, sign or visual—is foundational in fulfilling the Great Commission.
>
> 3. We affirm that the Bible is the Word of God, inspired, unchanging, and infallible. God's Word must be proclaimed to all nations, in every generation, every language, every platform, and every channel to accomplish the Great Commission of our Lord Jesus Christ.

4. We affirm the MAST Bible translation method as God's gift in supporting and complementing national efforts in doing Bible translation.

5. We affirm that God has called the local body of Christ in all nations of the world to advance Bible translation in every language and to be the final witness to the quality of God's Word translated in their heart language.

6. We affirm that God desires His glory to be declared among the nations through the preaching of His Word translated in all the languages of the nations, calling everyone to obedience, service, and transformation.

7. We affirm that God is equipping the global Church to utilize advances in knowledge, experience, and technology, and providing open access, ownership, propagation, and use of God's Word in the heart languages of the nations.

We are committed to work in synergy as members of the body of Christ to mobilize one another in various countries, denominations, parachurches, and like-minded associations to advance Bible translation to provide God's Word for all and as a legacy to future generations.

In response to the enthusiastic interest of these church leaders, we developed a program to train church leaders to lead MAST themselves. We call it Translation Education for National Training (TENT). The TENT curriculum covers the spiritual nature of Bible translation, an overview of Bible translation models, the eight steps of MAST, the educational theories underpinning MAST, technical support requirements, quality assurance, and workshop planning. We encourage these church partners to share all this training freely within their circles to expand global church capacity to translate and steward God's Word.

Since the original GCBT conference in Manila, we have hosted eleven more national and regional conferences and multiple TENT training events involving hundreds of church leaders. While the GCBT movement is just beginning, we understand that Bible translation has already begun in 50 more languages entirely under the leadership and coaching of these GCBT church partners!

What's Ahead

This year we are praying, planning, and working to see at least 715 languages begin Bible translation for the first time—almost two new languages every day!

The expansion of the Great Commission Bible Translation network and TENT training is creating the potential to see hundreds of new languages begin Bible translation through church initiatives that parallel and complement our own efforts. The 50 starts that have already occurred have been from a small number of churches. That number could easily triple or quadruple in the coming year. It could multiply ten-fold soon thereafter. Within a few years, this combination of efforts could yield thousands of new translations.

Although new starts are not the goal, they are obviously pre-requisite to having complete Bibles translated and accessible to the people. Once started, the pace of translation prog-ress using MAST is primarily a function of how many bilin-gual translators are involved. Larger teams make greater progress, and the size of the team is entirely up to the local church. Translation quality is a function of community engagement, church leadership involvement, and access to high-quality references to assist in resolving translation dif-ficulties. Accessibility of translated Scripture means it may need to be in print, audio, video, and/or symbolic format (for blind/deaf communities).

By God's grace, we may see thousands of language groups with the complete Bible translated within just a few years. What will be the next priority? Our continuing priority will be to serve languages that are still without Scripture until there are none. But for the thousands of language groups that have the Bible, the next priority likely will be developing resources to increase their understanding of Scripture: Bible studies, concordances, dictionaries, and historical references. Some of these resources may be translated from majority languages. Others will be produced within the minority language groups. Serving these minority language churches will be a continuing opportunity for all of us.

God's Story

The Sawi story is fundamentally God's story. In their hopelessness, He kindled hope. He placed a redemptive analogy, the peace child exchange, into their violent culture to prepare for His peace. He sent His ambassadors, Don Richardson and his family, to proclaim the gospel. God also sent other Christians from the U.S., Canada, the Papuan highlands, and other regions of Indonesia to encourage and instruct the Sawi in their faith. God sovereignly gave His Word, in the New Testament, to the Sawi and used it to raise and strengthen three generations of Sawi Christians. He is now enabling them to translate the Old Testament and steward His Word for themselves.

The amazing reality today is that, like the Sawi, thousands of other language groups are also providentially prepared to translate and steward God's Word. The Sawi are not a unique exception—they are a reflection of the preparation God has been making in churches across the globe. Other minority groups have vastly different cultures, languages, and history. But God has been at work preparing them for His Word.

> After this I looked and there before me was
> a great multitude that no one could count,
> from every nation, tribe, people and language,

standing before the throne and in front of the Lamb. They were wearing white robes and were holding palm branches in their hands. And they cried out in a loud voice: "Salvation belongs to our God, who sits on the throne, and to the Lamb" (Revelation 7:9-10).

Each of us can share in making this vision become a reality in our lifetime.